Hunt The Grunnock

Stage One

by Michael Roberts
with illustrations by Peter Hearsey

Sponsored by

ST CHRISTOPHER

The Traveller's Friend
for over 30 years

The Great St Christopher Grunnock Hunt

After centuries of seclusion, hidden away in a secret valley in the wilds of Scotland, the last of the grunnocks have been spotted again.

Recently their hideaway was discovered by the Ghastly Grunnock Grabbers. All they want to do is to capture and kill a grunnock. By a stroke of good fortune, Young Kit (the younger brother of St. Christopher, the patron saint of travellers) found a secret tunnel built centuries earlier. With his friends who you will meet in this book, he managed to help the Great Grunnock, the last Chieftain of the tribe, to escape.

But the Ghastly Grunnock Grabbers are now in hot pursuit of the gallant band of heroes. They have one chance. If you can help the Thump family find a new secret hideaway then the grunnocks might be saved. As the Thump family drive around Britain, they have to solve various clues. When put together they will point to a place in Britain where the grunnocks will be safe – at least for a time.

You can help them. Discover the the secret hideaway before the Ghastly Grunnock Grabbers, and you can save the Great Grunnock and his friends.

It will be tough. It will test your skill. But it will be FUN.

Illustrations: Peter Hearsey   Design & Layout: CE Marketing
Printed by: Kent Edwards Litho Ltd

The Reward

Message from the Great Grunnock via 'Haggiflyer-post'

Never forget that Hunting the Grunnock is a FUN HUNT to help you while away the time while travelling on Britain's busy roads. If enough of you are really keen, then the hunt will continue with new Stages in new Booklets. To build up the prize, for every Great Grunnock booklet sold the publishers will, at their sole discretion, put 5% of the selling price into my 'Great Grunnock Treasure Chest'

There is already £5,000 in there!

So get your friends and family to join you in the Hunt to find a safe haven for me. Then you can swop your Grunnock Cards (see over page), fill up your wall chart more quickly, find me sooner **and help to build the prize in my treasure chest until it is absolutely grunormous!!**

Oh, Grunnocks!! Sorry, nearly forgot. Don't forget to get all the drivers in your family to help you solve the clues – **and you can explain to them how St.Christopher can help them keep driving (it tells you in the book).**

Good luck – and please save me soon.

Signed:- His Extraordinary Grunnockness

(His Mark)

How to 'hunt the grunnock'

There will be a number of Stages in the Great St Christopher Grunnock Hunt. A new Stage will be published quarterly*. **This booklet is Stage One.** Stage Two is planned to start in December*.

Answers to all the clues can be found in any good road atlas. You do not have to travel anywhere, except (if you so choose) to places where you might be able to collect extra Grunnock Cards in later Stages.

All you have to do is to follow the crazy adventures of the Thump Family as they Hunt the Grunnock with you.

Each clue is to a town or location marked in your road atlas. Once you have found the answer to a clue you must keep a letter. When you get to the end of each Stage, re-arrange the jumbled letters into their correct order and you will discover a new hideaway for the Great Grunnock and his strange bunch of friends.

You will meet many oddball creatures along the way, from the Hairy McHaggis to Caradoc the Unpredictably Invisible Dragon. These could be Friends of the Great Grunnock – which you become as soon as you send in for your wall chart (see below), or they could be one of the Ghastly Grunnock Grabbers Gang. So, be careful and good hunting!

Please Note
*The Publishers reserve the right at any time not to publish further Stages of The Great Grunnock Hunt if, in their opinion, not enough Grunnock Hunters are on the trail and it is uneconomic to continue. The editor's decision at all times is final and no correspondence will be entered into.

Grunnock Cards

In the back of this booklet you will find 6 Grunnock Cards. This is your starter pack. Every Grunnock Hunt Stage Booklet will contain 6 assorted Grunnock Cards.

You can collect more Grunnock Cards:-
* In the back of any Great Grunnock Hunt Booklet
* Direct from St. Christopher when you order your wall chart
or
* When your personal driver becomes a Friend of St. Christopher (see over).

There are 144 cards to collect in total.

They include all the Friends of the Great Grunnock as well as all the Ghastly Grunnock Grabbers Gang and they will help you find where the Great Grunnock Treasure Chest is hidden.

You can order your wall chart with this Booklet (see back of book) and add your Grunnock cards as you collect them.

Important note.
To stand a chance of winning the major prize you need to collect ALL the cards, solve the clues in all the Stages to find where the Treasure Chest is and one member of your family must become a member of St. Christopher (who is there to protect all travellers, especially those who drive on the roads in Britain).

ST CHRISTOPHER
The Traveller's Friend
for over 30 years

Licensed to Drive

Are you still?

St. Christopher is the Patron Saint of travellers. He helps them reach their destination safely.

St.Christopher will also help you to find the Great Grunnock and his Treasure. His younger brother Young Kit, who is only 947 years old, is going to guide you on the Hunt in these booklets while you and your family drive around Britain, either on business, on a fun day out or while you are on holiday.

How?

Very simply.

To drive you need a licence and, however careful and sensible a driver is, sometimes things go wrong and they can lose their licence. St. Christopher strongly disapproves of dangerous or reckless driving but, if a driver loses his licence for speeding or 'totting up', St. Christopher can help. You will see how as you Hunt the Grunnock.

The legend of the Great Grunnock

S omewhere, deep in the heart of darkest Britain, the lost tribe of the Grunnocks has a secret hideaway. Few people have seen them and even fewer have actually caught one. Colonel Blowen is one of those people, known to serious Grunnock Hunters as "He who travels in the wind."

Excerpt From The Diary Of Colonel Blowen

Many years ago I stopped to ask directions from an ancient yokel.
"Are ye from around here?" he asked, in a quavering voice.
"No," I replied. "That's why I am asking for directions."
"Aar, I thought as much." He shot out an arm, a long, bony finger pointing to where a narrow road disappeared into the swirling mountain mist. "Ye go thataway, stranger."

Doubtfully, I eyed the direction he indicated. The twisting track looked far from inviting. But when I turned to question the old man, he had gone. There was nothing for it. I turned the car and drove deep into the mountains. Soon, I was totally lost in the mist. Suddenly, with no warning, the road ended in a terrifying drop. I jammed on the brakes. Cutting the engine, I wound down the window and listened. I could hear nothing but the roar of water. I clambered out and crept gingerly to the edge of the precipice. A hundred feet below me, an angry torrent thundered down a rocky gorge. A sudden flicker of headlights made me turn. My car was rolling towards the edge!

Helpless to prevent the catastrophe, I watched in stunned disbelief as the car toppled over and fell into the maelstrom below. I was alone in the wild darkness. Alone? Well, not entirely it seemed. Somebody or something had released the handbrake on my car.

As anger gave way to despair, I found myself shivering with cold. I had to get out of that place or I would die of exposure.

I don't know how many hours I scrambled through that hellish landscape but finally I sank down exhausted against a fallen tree. Almost unconscious, I heard a faint scratching sound close by. Then a piteous cry pierced the air. I summoned the last reserves of my energy and crawled around the tree trunk.

An amazing sight confronted me. A small, almost spherical pink creature, lay trapped, one leg caught beneath a splintered branch. A pair of huge, watery eyes gazed up fearfully. A single sharp tooth protruded from the front of a wide mouth. It looked like nothing I had ever seen – a kind of bladder with attitude. It whined again.

After much heaving I managed to lift the branch enough to release the trapped leg. Whimpering, the creature scrambled out. For a moment it regarded me solemnly, then blinked and hopped away.

Totally exhausted, I remember little of what followed. It was almost as if I was in a dream. I recall being lifted and carried through the trees. Voices drifted in and out of my hearing. Some of the words I understood, others were in some ancient language.

'... **helped me...**

kill him... mortal danger... only a human... just because... glurk... spooflekrunch... yeurcgh yeurcgh yeurcgh ...

put us all in peril... he will tell... humans will find ...'

I remember a deep valley, strangely luxuriant in the wild, bare mountains. Then a warm burrow of soft dry earth, lined with bracken. I slept, woke and slept again. At one point there appeared to be a meeting of some kind. Strange shapes gathered around a campfire. Some round and hairless but others were different. And behind them something huge lurked in the shadows. Voices were raised in argument. In the end, the small creature I had rescued seemed to win the day and my life was spared.

The next thing I remember is waking up in a bus shelter outside the Glenurqhart Lodge Hotel by Loch Ness. I was hungry, filthy and with a strange reek about me that I identified as goat-droppings.

Still ringing in my ears were the words: 'Always forget, a true grunnock never remembers'. I feel it may have lost something in the translation.

Editors' Note: -
Colonel Blowen spent the next few years in and out of special care units. When allowed out he would head immediately into the mountains, often scantily clad and on an ancient racing bicycle, to continue his search for the lost grunnock tribe and, in particular, the Great Grunnock. His scribbled notes were found by his bedside after he disappeared for the final time on New Year's Eve, 2001. He has not been seen since.

Notes Found Beside
Colonel Blowen's Bed

Anyone reading these notes must believe they are true, although I know my story can scarcely be credited.

The facts are these. Following my first encounter with Grunkle, (for that was the name of the grunnock I rescued), I met with the tribe on a number of occasions and learned the reason for their secretive ways. Their deepest fear was that the Ghastly Grunnock Grabbers would discover them, kill them all and convert their remains into firelighters, foghorns, fridge magnets, fairy-cake icing and flip-flop grease – a fate to inspire the profoundest terror.

Two weeks ago, the worst happened. The dreaded Grabbers finally found The Secret Valley. The slaughter was terrible. Very few grunnocks escaped, but those that did managed to take their chieftain, the Great Grunnock, with them. Since that dreadful night there has been no sign of them.

If the Great Grunnock can be found and kept safe then the tribe will survive. Otherwise, their fate will be unimaginably horrible. I am leaving tonight to find them. I believe that they are heading for the Sacred Grunnock Grove where the Great Grunnock's Treasure Chest lies buried. I am sure that is what the Ghastly Grunnock Grabbers are REALLY after.

Signed
Arbogast Blowen – Col. (retd.)
Blowen "In the wind"

P.S. Sorry, I forgot to mention a few Grunnock facts.

A grunnock thinks of nothing else but filling its stomach. They naturally gravitate towards food sources and may leave clues to their whereabouts.

Ghastly Grunnock Grabbers try to trap grunnocks by adopting the ancient Haggis-Hunter's trick of digging pits and baiting them with 'neeps'. This is odd because grunnocks actually loathe neeps. But if you see or smell neeps be extra careful.

Watch out for 'flashing cameras'! Don't rush and get caught for speeding. You could lose your licence and then you'd stand no chance of finding the Grunnock treasure!

The Challenge

There are 15 clues on Stage One of the Great St. Christopher Grunnock Hunt. Each clue will provide you with one letter or possibly with a hyphen or an apostrophe that together form the place name you are seeking. The clues are not in sequence.

The answer you are looking for has fifteen letters or hyphens/apostrophes etc and is the name of the place where The Great Grunnock is currently thought to be hiding.

However, all the letters are mixed up. You must solve all the clues then unravel the answer. It may (or may not) be more than one word. The answer will be found in Great Britain.

At any time you can send off for the Secret Grunnock Grove Wallchart on which to stick your Grunnock Cards. (See order form in back of this book).

Important Notice
Only when you have found the correct answers to all the Stages in all the booklets and you have collected all the cards will you be able to find the final location of the Sacred Grunnock Grove. You will then have to answer one final question/clue and you could win the most Grunmuncheous Prize ever.

Another Important Notice
There is absolutely no need to dig or pass across any private land. The actual site where The Great Grunnock may be is a place name. You only need to use a road atlas and a brain!

Good luck and don't fall into any Grunnock-Traps. Some have been set!

Contents

| | The legend of the Great Grunnock | 7 |
| | Notes found beside Colonel Blowen's bed | 9 |

Chapter 1	The terrible slaughter	15
Chapter 2	In which we meet the Thumps	19
Chapter 3	In which all is explained to the Thump family	22
Chapter 4	The hunt is on	25
Chapter 5	Drone joins the gang	27
Chapter 6	A close encounter	30
Chapter 7	We meet Sam the Eagle	33
Chapter 8	Hurricane in trouble	35
Chapter 9	Enter the neeps	38
Chapter 10	Things happen Roundabout 'ere	41
Chapter 11	Satchmo the Irrit joins the hunt	43
Chapter 12	Mr Thump in trouble	45
Chapter 13	Thud learns how to og a neep	48
Chapter 14	Bookworm Knowitall solves the problem	51
Chapter 15	The first battle	54
Chapter 16	Nabbed!	58
Chapter 17	Over the briny	61
Chapter 18	Banned!	64
Chapter 19	We all live in a UWV submarine	67
Chapter 20	Viking memories	70
Chapter 21	Overhauled by the enemy	73
Chapter 22	The second great battle	76
Chapter 23	Punctuation	80
Chapter 24	Nessie to the rescue	83

	Finding the Great Grunnock	86
	St Christopher Application Form	89

The Characters

Here is the list of all the characters involved in this Stage of
The Great St Christopher Grunnock Hunt

The Main Players
The Great Grunnock hisself. Extremely rare. Only one known
Grunlings – baby grunnocks. Also rare and often extremely noisy
Young Kit – St Christopher's younger brother
St Christopher – knew Marco Polo well. Often to be found helping
travellers. Especially those blinded by the 'flash' of a speed camera

Grunnock Hunters
Mr Thump (Dad)
Minnie Thump (Mum) – his wife
Slip – daughter
Thud – son
Crunch – toddler. Not rare and often extremely noisy
Patience Driver – who comes to the rescue of the Thumps
Colonel Blowen

Friends Of The Great Grunnock
The whole Haggis tribe... including:

Wee Angus McHaggis
The Huge Haggis (aka The Great Dumpling)
Hurricane the Haggiflyer
Drone the Haggipiper
The Hairy McHaggis
Hank McHaggis (the fastest og-shooter in the world)

Plus
Bookworm Knowitall
Satchmo the Irrit
Muncho – a small irrit (unqualified)
Sam the follicly-challenged American eagle
Caradoc the unpredictably invisible Dragon

Sir Loin Mediumrare – Sir Loin was a beefeater at the Tower of London before he was caught eating a salad sandwich during lunch break. He had the rare experience of being thrown *out* of the Tower.
Ollyphant (a strange cross between an elephant and a squid)
A Grunnock Fettling stick (For fettling grunnocks)
Various ogs and neeps
PC Bloodhound
Sergeant Mole

The Ghastly Grunnock Grabbers Gang

Horace Hogsnout – who is actually a Hairy Haggis-Hunter
Duckbilled Sourpuss
Sourpuss's attendant peripatetic thundercloud
Roundabout 'ere – A wandering roundabout
Genghis 'Flash' Gofast
Whinjer
Whiner
The Dark and Dingy Ones – about whom little is known (yet).

To discover what the Great Grunnock actually looks like you will need to collect all the Grunnock Cards and stick them on to the wall chart of the Secret Grunnock Grove.

GRUNNOCK PARTS

What do Grunnocks look like? For your eyes only, here is a sneak preview of certain selected parts of the Great Grunnock, himself. Keep this information secret!

CHAPTER ONE

The terrible slaughter

It was dawn when the Ghastly Grunnock Grabbers came howling out of the mist and launched their devastating attack on the valley. The grunnocks, many of whom had never seen humans before, were caught completely unawares. They didn't stand a chance.

The Grabbers' leader, Sourpuss, directed operations from the top of a convenient rock. He was a large mottled-green duck. Watching the mayhem, his slitty eyes glittered with evil pleasure and drool dripped from his twisted beak. Strangely, his purple warty webbed feet stood in a growing pool of water. A small black thundercloud hung over his head, constantly drenching him with rain. Every now and again a shaft of lightning struck a bald, scarred patch on his head, giving him, a violent and frightening twitch.

"Grab 'em,' screamed Sourpuss, whirling his wickedly sharp cleaver above his head. The cloud dodged the swing and crackled ominously.

For all their clumsiness and cowardice, the Grabbers could hardly fail. Wielding huge nets, they scooped up the terrified grunnocks and flung them into sacks. The evil laughter of the Grabbers and the terrified squeals of grunnocks and grunlings filled the valley.

Those that tried to escape did not get far. A vast mound of festering neeps blocked every path out of the valley. Faced with this awful stench, all the grunnocks collapsed into trembling heaps and were quickly captured by the pursuing Grabbers.

Young Kit, the younger brother of St

Evil mastermind, Duckbilled Sourpuss

Christopher (the traveller's friend) was visiting his grunnock friends to celebrate his 947th birthday. He had been the first to spy the Grabbers as they burst out of the mist. Luckily, they hadn't spotted him. If they had, they would have seen a hippie-style figure in robes and beads with long curly black hair. Normally, his face wore a friendly smile, but not today. He crouched down behind a tussock, hardly daring to breathe as huge hobnailed boots thundered past him. From his place of concealment he watched, horrified, as the Grabbers went about their dastardly work. Fiercely, he racked his brains. The awful smell of neep was making his head swim. He had to get out of here. But how?

Suddenly, an idea occurred to him. He leapt to his feet and started running, his robes fluttering behind him. Keeping low, he worked his way round behind the attackers to where two of his trusted friends (who had also come to the valley to help celebrate his birthday) stood gazing stupidly at the carnage. He grabbed them and pulled them behind a rock.

"Listen, you lummoxes," he whispered urgently. "We have to save the Great Grunnock. Keep your heads down and stick with me."

Totally bemused by the terrible events around them, Wee Angus (a haggis of the McHaggis tribe) and Caradoc (a scarlet Welsh dragon) scampered after Young Kit. Using the gorse as cover, they slipped through the mist from hummock to hummock until they reached the Grand Burrow. They dived in and landed in a heap on top of the massive bulk of the Great Grunnock himself.

"Ooomph! What do you think you're ...?"

"No time for that, Your Great Loftiness," broke in Kit. "We're under attack." Rapidly, he explained the situation.

What Kit had remembered amidst the panic and confusion was that the Grand Burrow held the means to escape. Built thousands of years before, it had a secret tunnel that led to the outside world. While Caradoc hung onto the Great Grunnock to prevent him

Young Kit on his 947th birthday

dashing into battle and certain death, Kit fought to to make him see reason. Meanwhile, Wee Angus was grabbing some essential supplies and stuffing them into his gubbins bag.

"Time to beat a strategic retreat, your Elevatedness," Kit whispered urgently. "For the sake of all Grunnockdom, we need to get you away from here."

The Great Grunnock peered out of the burrow-entrance at the terrible scene in the valley. "We'll have our revenge," he growled. He shuffled over to a chest and pulled out an ancient and very dusty chart. "If I can find my Treasure Chest in the Sacred Grunnock Grove it will lead us to the Even More Secret Valley. We'll be safe there and can plan our retaliation."

"Maybe," said Kit coughing in the dust as he hustled him towards the mouth of the tunnel. "But right now we have to concentrate on survival."

It was several hours before the Ghastly Grunnock Grabbers realised that their main prize had escaped. By that time the little band was stowed away on a goods train heading for London. It was cold in the open wagon, so Caradoc kept them warm with a steady flame from his nostrils. Kit got on his mobile phone and rang ahead for help.

"Um, I don't want to appear rude," said Wee Angus to the Great Grunnock. "But why do you need a chart to show you the way to your Treasure Grove, anyway. Don't you remember?"

The Great Grunnock looked surprised by the question. "Because every now and again it shifts its location, of course. Security and all that, see?"

"Ah, right," said Wee Angus, who didn't see at all.

On the station they were met by Sir Loin Mediumrare. Tall, thin, pale and wearing a slightly harrassed expression, you'd never guess from his appearance that he was was a beefeater who had just been sacked from the Tower of London for sneaking a salad in his lunch hour.

"How's the vegetarian life?" asked Kit.

"Don't ask," snorted Sir Loin. "I got the car you wanted, and here's the road atlas."

The Great Grunnock grabbed it and laid his ancient chart over the big map of Britain in the front. The chart was so worn and thin with age that the modern map showed through. "Show us the way to my Treasure Chest," he demanded.

Slowly, a dot appeared on the chart. Caradoc peered at it. "Dartford would that be?"

Wee Angus's eyes widened. "How does it work?" he asked.

"No time right now," broke in Kit, before the Great Grunnock could launch into an explanation. "Tell us later".

Quickly they thanked Sir Loin and bundled into the car. None of them noticed the ratty-looking individual who was watching them from behind a pillar. He was talking excitedly into his mobile phone. Sourpuss had agents everywhere.

Kit took the wheel and drove eastwards through the darkened streets. Consulting the ancient chart as they went, they followed the road through Dartford, Chatham, Sittingbourne and then via Dunkirk to Canterbury, all the while keeping an eye out for the Grunnock Grabbers.

Dawn found them still heading east.

Caradoc made use of the daylight to examine the Great Grunnock's chart. "I'm foxed," he admitted finally. "I thought I knew a bit about invisibility – it's my speciality. But I don't understand how this works."

"Nor do I, young dragon," said the Great Grunnock cheerfully. "It was made many years ago by a member of our tribe called Gruntfettle who did jobs on the side for Merlin. Sometimes it just shows you your route. Sometimes it gives you clues. – but only one at a time. You have to find one location before you can go on to the next one."

"So the Secret Grove is somewhere near here in Kent?" asked Kit.

"Might be, might not. The chart rarely shows a direct route. Gruntfettle's little joke." He pointed at the chart where words were gradually becoming clear. "There's our first clue."

Caradoc in invisible mode

"'**Find the town that starts a game of cards...**'" read Wee Angus, "'**... and remove one letter to leave it sounding like a juvenile trotter.**' What's that supposed to mean?"

Everyone looked puzzled.

Suddenly, Kit laughed and pointed at a road sign. "There's the answer. Obvious when you think about it."

Light dawned on the faces of his companions.

"That's one of the letters we need to find my Treasure Grove," exclaimed the Great Grunnock. "Keep it safe, young Kit."

CHAPTER TWO

In which we meet the Thumps and the Haggiflyer

An hour later, the tired group stood round the car shivering in the mist. Dewdrops dripped from their chilly noses or, in Wee Angus's case, from his schmonker – schmonkers being the haggis equivalent of noses.

"Are we lost then, young Kit?" the voice of the Great Grunnock boomed.

"Please be quiet, Your Overarching Loftiness," whispered Kit. "We don't know where the Grabbers are hiding. They could be anywhere."

Huddling closer together, they peered nervously into the concealing mist.

Suddenly a voice echoed eerily above them.

"Tac-a-tac-a-tac-tac-a. Bandits at ten-o-clock! Climb to Angels one five."

"Oh no," sighed Wee Angus McHaggis. "It's my cousin, Hurricane the Haggiflyer."

"Isn't he friendly, then," asked Caradoc, puzzled.

"Friendly? Yes. Just accident-prone."

"Dashed thick cloud this. Uh-oh, no instruments! Prepare to crash land!"

"Duck, everyone."

"Oooomph!" exclaimed the Great Grunnock as the Haggiflyer thudded into his stomach.

"Oops, sorry, Your Towering Eminence, didn't see you lying there."

"Quiet, Hurricane!" Wee Angus whispered fiercely. "Grabbers raided the Grunnock's secret valley last night. They're after us. Have you seen them?"

The Haggiflyer shook his head. "Definitely not, old bean. Mind you, couldn't see much in this soup. Bit short on radar, you know?"

"How would radar help you?" snorted Wee Angus, "You can only fly backwards."

"Righto, jolly good show. Spot on." A cunning grin suffused his features and he tapped his schmonker for emphasis. "But just remember, I can clearly see where I've been. And if it's of any interest to you, young fellow, there are some lights coming straight towards us." He pointed into the mist. The little band turned to run just as a pair of headlights flared out of the gloom.

Hurricane the Haggiflyer

Suddenly, they jerked sideways. With a loud grating of gears followed by an ear-splitting squeal of brakes, the car skidded to a halt. The caravan it was towing slewed round and pinned the Great Grunnock against a tree.

Mr Thump opened the car door. He was a large shambling sort of man with a distracted air. He looked around and scratched his head.

"Strange. Thought we'd clipped something then."

"We did, Dad," exclaimed his son Thud as he clambered out of the back door. "Look over there." He pointed to Caradoc who was fading in and out of sight like a flickering light bulb.

"My fault," admitted the dragon, ruefully. "You couldn't have seen my tail. It was invisible. So you ran into it. Think you clipped my dematerialiser sensitive spot. Expect it'll settle down in a minute."

"Oh my goodness!" exclaimed Mrs Thump "What on earth is that?"

"A dematerialiser sensitive spot? Well it's …"

"No, I mean what on earth are you?"

"It's obviously a dragon, Mum, anyone can see that. And not a very impressive one at that." The voice, accompanied by a loud sigh, came from Slip, her teenage daughter who was sitting in the back of the car, an air of bored resignation on her face.

Caradoc opened his mouth to protest but, just then, with a loud roar of indignation, the Great Grunnock squeezed out from behind the caravan and peered in at Mrs Thump's window.

Mrs Thump promptly fainted.

"Mum's having one of her turns again," yelled Thud.

"I'm not surprised," gasped Mr Thump. "What on earth is going on here?"

Just then, Kit glimpsed something through the swirling mist. "Quiet everyone. UWV incoming".

"UWV…what on…mmmmmnngh." A huge hand with strange fingers wrapped itself around Mr Thump's mouth. Everyone stood silently in the mist as they listened to the sound of an approaching vehicle.

CHAPTER THREE

In which all is explained to the Thump family

Wee Angus the haggis tapped the Great Grunnock on a leg. "Ease off a bit, your Enormousness. He's going a bit purple." The Great Grunnock peered down in surprise. Slowly he loosened his grip but held a sucker to his mouth in a gesture to silence the apoplectic human.

Young Kit moved in quickly. "Don't say a word. They're just the other side of the bushes." He pointed as the sound of the engine died away. "By the way, a UWV is a Ubiquitous White Van," he whispered. "They're taking over the motorways. Haven't you noticed?"

Mr Thump nodded blankly, his eyes staring at the strange creatures around him. His wife, Minnie, had come round and was moaning quietly in the front seat. In the back, Slip was pointedly ignoring everyone and reading her magazine. Beside her, Crunch the toddler slept on in his car seat. Thud was staring with interest at Caradoc who was frantically trying to find a way to stop popping in and out of sight.

"This is the spot. Keep quiet and listen," a voice hissed menacingly in the mist.

"Nah! I reckon they've gone, Boss."

"Shuddup, Whinjer. Either they're here or I'm not the Duckbilled Sourpuss."

"But that's what you are, Boss," came another snivelling whine.

"Idiot, Whiner. Of course I am. That's why I said … Oh, forget it, numbskull."

"I'm not sure that our two comrades have been graced with the necessary in the brain box area to understand the gist of your genius, Sourpuss." The third voice was soft and silky and laced with menace.

"I know that voice," whispered Hurricane. "That's Genghis Gofast, aka 'Flash' Gofast. Gets his kicks from tearing along roads tripping the speed cameras. He's one crazy pilot you don't want to meet the wrong way down a dual carriageway."

"Ssshhh." Wee Angus frowned at Hurricane.

"I smell something else." Another voice like wheels crunching gravel broke the silence.

Wee Angus shivered. "That's Horace Hogsnout," he whispered. "He's a Haggis Hunter, the worst of the lot. If he's in league with Sourpuss we're in serious trouble."

The silence lengthened. Crunch stirred in his sleep and opened an eye.

"Humph," Sourpuss's voice crackled through the silence. "Maybe you're right. Maybe they aren't here. But we've got to get that map and find that treasure before the Great Grunnock. If we fail, the Dark and Dingy Ones will have us for breakfast."

"Too right, Boss," whined Whinjer. "If …" Their voices were drowned by the roar of the engine. With a squeal of tyres the UWV thundered out of the trees and onto the road. The sound faded into the distance.

"Phew. That was a close one," muttered Caradoc.

"Excuse me." Mr Thump spoke in a slightly shaky voice. "Would somebody mind telling me what's going on here?"

"Of course. Very remiss of us." Young Kit rapidly performed introductions that only left the Thumps looking at each other in confusion. He glanced sideways at the Great Grunnock and nodded meaningfully towards the caravan. "And then there's me," he continued. " You may have heard of my big brother St Christopher – you know the one – The Traveller's Friend – looks after all you drivers on the roads of Britain…" Mr Thump nodded dazedly. "Well, big Bro said to find a really nice family who can help us find the Secret Grunnock Grove…"

"The what?" exclaimed Mrs Thump.

"His Secret Grove." Young Kit jerked a thumb over his shoulder to where the Great Grunnock and the rest of the band were just disappearing into the caravan.

"Hey. Just a moment," exclaimed Mr Thump "You can't do that you know. We've got to…"

"…save the country. That's what you've got to do," interrupted Young Kit. "Look. Please. We need your help. We have to get the GG to his treasure in the Secret Grunnock Grove before Sourpuss and his band."

"Who are these Dark and Dingy Ones they mentioned?"

"Don't know for sure," admitted Kit. "Only rumours. But put it this way: if Sourpuss is frightened of them, they have to be mega-evil. If we can only get to the Grove first, you'll get some of the treasure as a reward. Then we can hide the rest in The Even More Secret Valley and put it out of reach of the Dark and Dingy Ones for ever." He looked earnestly at the Thumps. "If you don't help us we're really stuck. What do you say?"

"Oh, come on Dad," urged Thud. "It'll be uberkool to save the country. You've not done that yet, have you? Have you?"

Mr Thump realised he was the centre of attention. The anxious faces of Wee Angus, Caradoc and Hurricane peered at him through the caravan's window. The GG's head stuck out of the roof but the big watery eyes that were visible begged him to say yes.

He sighed. "I don't appear to have much option. Where are we going?"

"Hurrah!" An ear-splitting cheer drowned the sound of the engine.

CHAPTER FOUR

The hunt is on

Mrs Thump, who had introduced herself as Minnie, rested the road atlas on her knees. She was looking in consternation at Gruntfettle's chart.

"But there's nothing on it," she exclaimed. "How can I possibly navigate to the next clue?"

"Be patient, O Beauteous One," boomed the GG's voice through the open sun-roof. Mr Thump rolled his eyes to the heavens as Minnie Thump blushed a deep pink. Her spectacles fogged over with emotion. "The next clue will appear – or part of it, at least. If we go in the wrong direction the chart will give off a foul odour."

"Sounds like Crunch to me," muttered Slip. "He's always giving off…"

"That'll do, dear," said her Dad quietly.

Minnie looked at the map closely.

"Oh, now I can see. It says… **'Follow the A258 past a town after which a flatfish is named and take the motorway to where a tree stands by a shallow river crossing.'**

"I know that one," said Thud excitedly. "Look, there it is." He pointed at a spot where the road atlas showed through the map.

"Well done son, now we're on the right road. Where to next?"

Minnie peered at the map. Another sentence suddenly appeared.

"This is fun," she said.

"Well I don't think it is," grumbled Slip. "I'm starving and I think Crunch has had an accident again!"

"All right dear, we'll stop at the next Little Chef we see and have some lunch." She turned back to the map. "It says here…**'Now take the A28, A262 and**

Minnie Thump, ace map-reader

A21 which will lead you to another water crossing – this one made from barrels and fit for a monarch. We need the second letter of the barrel bit."' She frowned. "It also says we can fettle a grunnock here if required."

Thud looked up through the sun-roof. The GG's head swayed above in time with the motion of the caravan.

"Do you need fettling yet Mr Grunnock?" he enquired.

"Not yet, but thank you kindly for asking," the grunnock replied smiling broadly.

Mr Thump shifted uncomfortably and looked sideways at his wife.

"I'm not totally sure we're doing the right thing," he said. "How on earth does one 'fettle' a grunnock?"

"I'm sure Mr Grunnock will tell us when it is necessary," replied Minnie primly. "Meanwhile, I think I've worked out where we should be headed. Take the next left please."

While Dad drove, Minnie explained her thinking to Kit, who nodded enthusiastically. "That's the letter I need to remember," he agreed.

The mist had cleared and they made good time on the almost empty roads.

As they were approaching their destination, the Great Grunnock stuck his head in through the sun-roof and sniffed. "You sure we're still on course?" He enquired with a worried expression; "There's certainly a bit of a pong coming from somewhere!"

"Mum," complained Slip, "Crunch is not nice to know!"

Just at that moment they saw the sign for a Little Chef and, with a squeal of tyres Mr Thump swung into the car park. Behind him the GG and friends tumbled in a heap on the floor of the caravan.

Thud, holding his nose with his fingers, flung open the back door and scrambled out. His feet landed on something very squelchy which let out a loud and mournful wail.

CHAPTER FIVE

Drone joins the gang

Ouch. Watch where you're putting your Beetlecrushers." "Ooops. Sorry," said Thump. He looked wide-eyed at the small creature at his feet. It was like a long sausage with pipes sticking out of it. And it was covered all over in a rather fetching tartan.

"Hi, Drone," said Wee Angus. "What brings you so far south?"

"Oh, hello Angus and…" Drone stared up at the Great Grunnock towering above. " …uh..and yourself, Sir." He moved stiffly on short legs. A tuneless droning sound came from his pipes. "I'm meant to be looking after The Huge Haggis," he explained. "Those Sassenach Haggis Hunters are on our trail still, and I'm trying to get him into hiding before Burns' Night."

"Well, you'd better join us then. We're on the run as well – from the Ghastly Grunnock Grabbers."

"Great idea," replied Drone, looking pleased, "but easier said than done. The HH disappeared into that Little Chef two hours ago. You know what that means!"

"Not just a light snack, then?"

"Could be," admitted Drone. "It's just that HH's idea of a light snack would keep a stable of sumo wrestlers fed for a week."

Drone, the Haggipiper

"Well, I need to sort little Crunch out," said Minnie Thump.

"And we're starving," said Slip and Thud in unison.

"Okay everybody." Mr Thump clapped his hands. "Let's all go and get something to eat before we get back on the road, and you can introduce us to your new friend."

Wee Angus quickly introduced Drone the Haggipiper to the assembled company and the whole group trooped into the Little Chef. Hurricane was persuaded to circle above the restaurant, keeping an eye out for Grabbers – but not before Wee Angus had promised to bring him out a haggi-bag of provisions.

"Not exactly quiet is he?" murmured Thud to his sister as the Haggipiper wheezed and groaned noisily as it bounced along.

Slip sniffed. "I'm not particularly bothered. They're your friends."

The customers and waitresses looked on in astonishment as the strange group entered the restaurant.

"Smoking or non-smoking?" asked the pretty waitress gazing up nervously at the GG. "Or perhaps you would like to sit with your friend over there?" She pointed.

On the far side of the room a huge, round haggis was jammed securely between the table and window. The table was strewn with empty plates.

"HH!" roared the GG bounding across the room scattering chairs and customers in all directions. "Long time no see, cousin."

The Huge Haggis struggled to extricate himself from behind the table, finally managing it with a loud schlumpff. He embraced the Great Grunnock

His Massive Globularity, the Huge Haggis

enthusiastically. Seeing them together, it was apparent that while the GG's enormous size was in a vertical direction, the HH more than matched him horizontally. If you'd launched him into orbit, astronomers would be talking excitedly about a new asteroid.

"Cousin?" exclaimed Mr Thump putting his hand to his forehead. "How many other relatives are we going to be landed with?"

"Probably quite a few more, I'm afraid," admitted Wee Angus. "We haggises and grunnocks tend to stick together."

"Thump!" Minnie appeared at the door of the Ladies. "I need your help here. Bring the Disaster bag."

"Disaster bag?" Mr Thump looked bemused. "What on earth is …"

"Here you are, Dad," said Slip, who was not really as offhand as she sometimes sounded. She handed him a holdall she had brought in from the car. "Nappies," she explained, "and everything Mum needs to make Crunch nice to know again."

Muttering under his breath Mr Thump disappeared towards the toilets. By the time he and Minnie reappeared, everyone was tucking into their food. Peace reigned. But it was not to last.

Suddenly, Hurricane zoomed into the restaurant, snatched a doughnut from a startled Crunch and, with his mouth full, circled the room at high speed.

"Grrooful lashscoming …"

"For goodness sake, don't talk with your mouth full," admonished Mrs Thump.

Startled, Hurricane swallowed with a load gulp. But, unused to being reprimanded, he lost concentration and crash-landed into the debris in front of the Huge Haggis. French fries scattered everywhere.

"Sorry," he mumbled. "But old Sourpuss and his crew are heading this way fast. We need to get out immediately."

There was a stampede for the door. Bringing up the rear Mr Thump settled the bill with his credit card. When all the items the Huge Haggis had consumed were added in, the bill was as long as his forearm. He blanched as he saw the total.

"I hope we find that treasure quickly," he thought to himself, "if we're going to have many meals like this!" He ran over to the car.

"Quick," he said as he climbed in. "Which way to the next clue?"

Minnie placed the magic map over the atlas. **Find your way across weald, vale, down and plain to where the Romans kept themselves clean. This town of rugby fame becomes a cricket hitter when we take out the letter we need.**

"That's not too difficult," said Dad after a moment's thought. "At least, I know from the first part of the clue where we should be headed. But it's quite a drive. Everyone settle in, relax and enjoy the view.

CHAPTER SIX

A close encounter

Belching exhaust fumes, the dirty white van screeched to a halt in the car park of the Little Chef. Genghis Gofast climbed down, leaned against the bonnet, took off his large sunglasses and started polishing them with his handkerchief.

"So much for your informant's intelligence. Doesn't look like they're here," he sneered at the Duckbilled Sourpuss who was peering closely at the ground. "You looking for a nesting site or something?" he snorted derisively.

"One more bright comment from you and I'll fix it so you'll never drive again," snarled Sourpuss. "Get inside and find out if they've been here and, if so, when they left. Shift it!"

Abashed, Gofast slunk off towards the restaurant.

"And take those two imbeciles with you," Sourpuss shouted after him pointing at Whinjer and Whiner who were heading purposefully towards the children's play area.

Sourpuss wiped a drip from his beak. He glanced up at the small black cloud that hovered above his head. "Don't even think about it," he snarled. The cloud always followed Sourpuss wherever he went, changing tone from dark grey to black depending on Sourpuss's mood. Mostly it stayed black. The angrier Sourpuss became, the denser the cloud and the more it rained on him. When he really lost it the cloud would shoot bolts of lightning at the duck. This did nothing to restore his temper but it terrified the opposition and, anyway, the cloud enjoyed it!

"I smell 'aggis!" Sourpuss turned to see Horace Hogsnout the Haggis Hunter emerging from the back of the van. His nose twitched most alarmingly. The dew-drop that seemed a permanent addition to this feature of his ugly face, shivered. It was always threatening to fall off but never quite managed to pluck up the courage to let go.

"Spare me your obsession with haggises," rasped Sourpuss, "It's the grunnock that'll lead us to the treasure."

"Don't wet yourself you moth-eaten apology for a bird," retorted Horace. "If they've joined together then we've got twice as much chance of catching 'em. I can smell 'em, see." He sniffed loudly. Sourpuss grinned nastily. "I'm surprised you can smell anything the way you stink. It's like travelling with a load of rotting compost with you and those pesky neeps on board."

"Listen, vulture-breath …"

"That's enough!" screamed Sourpuss. The cloud suddenly expanded and released a bolt of lightning, at the same time drenching the duck with a thunderous shower.

"Aaagh…!" yelled Sourpuss, jumping around the car park. "I'll get you for that."

"Now I can smell singed duck as well as 'aggis," sneered Horace. "A bit more of that and you'll be ready barbecued!"

At that moment Gofast and the Grabbers came pelting out of the restaurant.

"We're only a few minutes behind them," shouted Gofast "Let's get moving and we'll catch them in no time."

"Don't think I'll forget this," rasped Sourpuss to the Haggis Hunter. "Now get in the van."

Without waiting to see if the others were aboard, Gofast slammed the engine into gear and shot out into the road. Whinjer and Whiner, who had been clambering in through the back doors swung out horizontally as the van careered around the corner. Angrily, Horace flung out a huge fist, grabbed them by their collars and hauled them inside.

Engine roaring, the van rocketed past a roadside camera. It flashed.

"Yo, flash away, baby, I'm on the road," Gofast yelled, punching the air.

Behind him, a smartly striped police car moved slowly out from a side road.

"Cor, see that?" PC Bloodhound asked, before cramming the last of his triple burger with all on into his mouth.

"Yup." Sergeant Mole peered after the rapidly disappearing van. "Reckon you can catch 'im?"

"Whggrgrmhh!" exclaimed Bloodhound, then swallowed his mouthful and tried again. "What me! They don't call me Schumacher Bloodhound for nothing."

"Who does?"

"Who does what?"

"Calls you Shoemaker Bloodhound then?"

PC Bloodhound stared at his colleague blankly.

"Well I does for one," he retorted.

"Okay then Mr Shoemaker.

Genghis "Flash" Gofast, motoring menace

Perhaps we should get after them then or do you need to wait for the start signal?"

"Nah. I can go anytime I…"

"Well go then!" shouted Sergeant Mole, raising his eyes to heaven.

With a squeal of tyres the police car shot out into the road and roared off around the bend. A few seconds later it returned, this time going in the same direction as the Grabber's van!

Long-suffering team leader, Mr Thump

CHAPTER SEVEN

We meet Sam the Eagle

The Thumps and their caravan full of the Great Grunnock's friends continued southwest. They had found the name of the town in the third clue and were now looking for the next one.

"It says… **'Your quickest route to the next clue is to brave the M5 south and let the A30 carry you on to a spot near the highest summit on Dartmoor'**… then it fades out again," said Minnie.

"It'll come in again when we get nearer, I'm sure," said Young Kit. Thud and Slip had been pushed into the rear facing seats while Young Kit sat in the back next to Crunch. So it was Thud who first spotted their pursuers. Suddenly he sat up and stared through the caravan windows as it swayed along behind them.

"Hey Dad, there's UWV behind. He's catching us."

Mr Thump looked in his wing mirror. Thud was right. The white van was rapidly closing the gap. As he watched, he caught the flash as Gofast set off another speed camera.

"He'll lose his licence the way he's driving," said Thud.

"Unfortunately, I have a funny feeling that's not going to stop him," replied Young Kit.

"Well, we certainly can't outrun him at the speed he's going," said Mr Thump worriedly.

"We don't have to, Mr T," said the Great Grunnock peering down through the sun roof. "We have a plan." He winked one of his front eyes and disappeared back into the caravan.

"What do you think they're going to do?" asked Minnie.

"Don't even ask dear," sighed her husband. "Let's just concentrate on keeping this menagerie on the road. Look, there's the M5 ahead."

With a caravan towing behind him, Mr Thud knew he had to brake in time to join the slip road but he hung on till the last possible moment.

"Dad, they're almost on us!" shouted Thud. Mr Thump glanced in his mirror. He could see 'Flash' Gofast grinning wickedly beneath his shades as he crouched over the steering wheel. Beside him, Sourpuss and Horace Hogsnout were urging him on. Suddenly their triumphant grins turned to horror as their filthy van tilted sharply over, turned on its side and slid forward in a screeching shower of sparks. As Kit and the kids watched, it careered past them at breakneck speed and shot under the motorway.

Gobsmacked by this unexpected turn of events, Mr Thump only just managed to swing hard left up the filter road and onto the motorway. The caravan swayed alarmingly but the GG and the Huge Haggis both leaned out hanging onto the sides to keep it on an even keel.

"Hey, cool," shouted Thud. "You'd make really great windsurfers!"

Whooping with delight, the motley band drove south down the motorway. In the distance behind, the flashing blue light marked where PC Bloodhound and Sergeant Mole were closing in on the Grabbers' van.

Mr Thump let out a big sigh. "Okay gang, we've got a bit of a start on them now. We'd better find this next clue quickly."

"Just coming up," exclaimed Minnie excitedly as she held Gruntfettle's chart over the atlas. **"Take a tour – but one without you – no? Yes? Whatever fits but it's 619 on our map. Keep one letter to make a cuppa."**

"Hmmm. That doesn't sound so easy," mused Kit. "Hello, what's up with Crunch?" The others turned to look. Crunch was staring up through the sunroof gurgling and pointing to where a huge pair of talons were curled over the edge of the roof. Attached to them, was a very large, fierce looking eagle, wearing a stars and stripes waistcoat, a pair of half-spectacles and with a very bald head.

"Howdy!" It said, leaning forward and peering into the car. "Met a buddy of yours up ahead. Strange crittur. Called hisself Hurricane. Said you guys were looking for the Grunnock treasure. That right?"

"Well yes, but…"

"Don't blabber sir. Can't stand blabber. To the point that's me. The name's Sam. En route from LA to NY. Slight miscalculation with the navigation. Soon have it right. Know exactly where I am down to the last four or five hundred miles, yessir." He tilted his head on one side. "Saw a big rock not far ahead. Told the Haggiflyer dude. Reckon that's your target. OK. Must fly. Need to get home for the World Series. Can't be much off course. See ya around."

With that, Sam spread a pair of huge wings and let the wind lift him gracefully into the air. At that moment, a large truck thundered past on the opposite carriageway. The downdraught caught the eagle in middair, swept him onto the top of the cab and held him flat, wings spread, against the roof.

"Now I know what they mean by spread-eagled." quipped Young Kit as the lorry disappeared behind them. He sighed. "I fear it will be some time before he gets home again, if the name on the side's anything to go by. That lorry's heading for Aberdeen!"

CHAPTER EIGHT

Hurricane in Trouble

So how did you do it?" asked Slip as Wee Angus sat down beside her. They were all crammed together sitting in the warmth of the caravan following supper. They had finally found the clue on Dartmoor – Sam's reference to a big rock helped – and had decided to get some rest for the night in a well-hidden lay-by.

"Do what?" asked the haggis, innocently.

"Flip the Grabbers' van over like that?"

The Great Grunnock laughed gruffly. "That was easy, young Slip. Caradoc volunteered to use his body like a ramp. We slipped him out onto the road while he was invisible. Gofast never even saw him and went straight up his back like a rocket."

A quiet chuckle came from the space under the window. "I'm a bit stiff now, mind," said the dragon, materialising in front of them and stretching his wings. "Look!" They all stared. Tyre-tracks led straight up the dragon's tail, continuing up his back almost to his shoulders.

"Don't want to have to do that too often," grinned Caradoc. "Leaves me feeling rather flat."

The caravan rocked with laughter.

Crafty little Wee Angus, the haggis

Thud yawned tiredly and turned to Kit. "Do you think the police will catch Gofast for speeding?"

"Certainly hope so, Thud," Kit replied. "And take his licence away for a long time. My big bro, St C doesn't like dangerous or stupid drivers. Me neither. Mind you, sometimes even very careful drivers like your Dad can get flashed. A couple of times and even he risks losing his licence for a time."

"Don't worry son, it won't happen to me," laughed Mr Thump.

"Better not to risk it if you ask me," said Kit. "Not just because we're after treasure. Like most drivers, you need your car to get you to work, take Thud and Slip to school, and pop down to the superstore to shop. You'd be lost without a licence."

"Well, can't do much about it, can I," replied Dad.

"You certainly can," said Kit. "Just call St C and he can make sure that you can afford to pay someone to drive you around if you do make a mistake. It's not a lot you know, and better to be safe than sorry."

"Ah well, we'll see. But I can't see me getting flashed – can you Minnie?"

"Well… I don't know about that dear. Sometimes you do get a little distracted and…"

"Yes, well, never mind." Mr Thump sounded irritated. "Come on kids. Time for bed. We've a long day tomorrow. It's only a guess, but this chart seems to want to send us all over the country."

Soon, the caravan was in darkness. Slip, who wasn't really interested in driving round to find some silly old treasure, cuddled up to Wee Angus who lay snuggled in her arms. He grinned contentedly. 'These humans aren't so bad really,' he thought. 'At least, the ones who don't want to eat you are all right!'

Young Kit gazed out of the window at the clouds scudding across the moon.

"Looks windy up there," he said. "I hope the Haggiflyer's okay."

"Worry not, strange person, young Hurricane is well trained in getting out of trouble," said the Huge Haggis from his position inside the food cupboard.

"And pretty darned good at getting into it as well" grumbled Drone the Haggipiper from on top of a wardrobe.

᠊ᠣᠯ ᠊ᡏᡁ ᠋ᡝᡲ 🕺 ᡝᡲ ᡏᡁ ᠊ᠣᠯ

Some way away to the north, the Grabber's van was parked inside a garage repair shop. The lights were blazing. At the front Whinjer and Whiner, arms and faces black with oil, had their heads under the bonnet. The clatter of spanners echoed in the cavernous space.

"… typical. Driving like a maniac…"

"... knew the engine couldn't take a hammering like that ..."

" ... what do they expect from us... miracles?"

"Get on with it you two losers and stop whinjing and whining," Genghis Gofast snapped angrily. He paced up and down in front of them, a worried look on his face. If they didn't get that engine going soon, he could be in bad trouble.

Above them, Hurricane peered through a skylight. He could see everything. If they couldn't mend the van tonight then the Great Grunnock and gang would be well on their way to safety ... and it didn't look as if those two idiots even knew which way to hold a screwdriver.

Satisfied, Hurricane took off backwards without looking as usual, ricocheted off a telegraph pole, bounced once on the roof, crashed through a window and landed slap in the embrace of 'Flash' Gofast.

Whinjer and Whiner shot up out of the engine, smashed their heads in unison into the bonnet and collapsed senseless onto the floor.

"Well, well, well," hissed Gofast triumphantly, "What do we have here?"

CHAPTER NINE

Enter the neeps

Hurricane lay trussed like a chicken in a smelly patch of oil in the corner of the garage. The chill light of dawn shone weakly through the dirty windows. Gofast was asleep, stretched out along the front seat of the van, his legs hanging out of the door. Whinjer and Whiner were still out cold.

Sourpuss, accompanied by Hogsnout, waddled up to Hurricane and stuck his twisted beak under the haggiflyer's schmonker.

"I will ask you just once more," he hissed. "Where are your friends heading today? And where is the Grunnock's treasure?"

"I shall tell you nothing," retorted Hurricane through clenched tooth. "You can have my name, rank and number only. That is, if I could remember my number. Anyway, I'm Pilot Officer…"

"Shaddup!" screamed Sourpuss, cringing as the cloud deluged him with rain. "I'll make you talk, you rancid lump of sausage meat."

"Sausage meat!" exclaimed Hurricane indignantly. "I'll have you know that… Gracious me!" He was interrupted by the sight of Whinjer rising vertically from the floor,

Horrible Haggis Hacker, Horace Hogsnout

still unconscious, floating gracefully across the garage and dropping silently in a tumbled mass of arms and legs into a pile of soggy, oil-drenched cardboard in a corner.

Sourpuss, frantically trying to see through the rainstorm that occupied his personal space, noticed nothing.

"Stop pussy-footing around," growled Horace Hogsnout. "This 'ere's an 'aggis. I know how to make 'im talk."

"Huh! You and whose army," Hurricane snorted derisively.

"No army, flyboy," leered the Haggis Hunter, "but I do 'ave a neep or two 'andy!"

Hurricane blanched. Neeps! He'd forgotten about them. Hogsnout strode to the back of the van and yanked the doors open. Hurricane bit his lip with his single pointy tooth. This was not so good! Out of the corner of his eye he saw Sourpuss splashing around in a puddle trying desperately to avoid the bolts of lightning firing down at him from his personal cloud.

On the other side of the garage Whiner suddenly floated off the ground, ending up with a muffled thump in the rubbish next to Whinjer.

'Strange,' thought Hurricane, but he didn't have time to expand the thought as a platoon of neeps suddenly appeared from behind the van. They marched purposefully towards him. The sweat rolled down his forehead. This was not going to be easy. Frantically he tugged and twisted, straining at his bonds – but they were too tight.

Horace Hogsnout chortled gloatingly. "Not so cock-a hoop now are we flyboy? Surprisin' what a neep or two can do to an 'aggis! Yikes. 'ere, wot's goin' on?" The last because, suddenly, the Haggis Hunter was ten feet in the air approaching the recumbent forms of his two henchmen in the mess of oily cardboard. He struggled helplessly as, like the spaceship in Close Encounters, he turned smoothly upside down. Unlike the spaceship, gravity suddenly seemed to kick back in.

Splat! He landed smack between them. Out cold for the moment.

Hurricane, bemused by what had just happened had a more serious problem on his mind. Neeps! The nasty creatures were now so close, their dreadful pong overwhelmed him. Eyes watering, he gasped for breath and wriggled further back into the corner.

Suddenly, a large eye appeared beside his head. It winked.

"Hang on boyo, soon have you out of here," whispered Caradoc. Dispatched by The Great Grunnock, he had been searching for the haggiflyer. Even with his inbuilt haggi-locator skills, it had taken him several hours. Finally, the blazing lights from the dingy garage had led him to the rescue in the nick of time.

Hurricane yelped as Caradoc directed a jet of flame at his bonds. The singed rope snapped and, within seconds, the haggiflyer and the dragon were out of the garage and heading into the morning sun. Below them, Hurricane spied the Thumps' car and caravan scooting north up the M5.

Caradoc scanned the horizon and hummed quietly to himself. "Home… I smell home."

A few minutes later, Hurricane was recounting the night's events to his friends.

"**Find the M4 and turn west across the bridge that sounds like a number between one and ten,**" interrupted Minnie Thump, who had the map open on her lap. "**Enter the land where dragons roam…**"

"Yes, yes, yes.!" chortled Caradoc with excitement.

"**Then keep heading west,**" continued Minnie, "**until north of the motorway you find a town that's famous for its enormous castle and tangy cheese.**"

Caradoc smiled and nodded.

"**Keep the final letter of the town's name,**" concluded Minnie.

᠅ ᠅ ᠅ ᠅ ᠅ ᠅ ᠅

Far behind the gallant band of treasure hunters, the Duckbilled Sourpuss finally found refuge from his personal thunderstorm beneath a cardboard box.

"Gofast!" he yelled. "Get that dratted van moving. We need to be out of here or the Dark and Dingy Ones will make mincemeat of us.

Gofast took one look at Sourpuss's expression and decided that this was not the moment to come out with a sarcastic remark. "Where to, boss?" he enquired as he started the engine.

"North, you numbskull."

"What makes you so sure?" asked Gofast mildly.

"Coz I'm the brains and you're just the wheel-man. Now shift it!"

Gofast shifted. Sourpuss and Horace got out their mobiles and started ringing round their contacts. It was only a matter of time before someone spotted the Thumps and their caravan.

Roundabout 'ere

CHAPTER TEN

Things happen roundabout 'ere

The Ghastly Grabbers Ubiquitous White Van screeched to a halt. Black exhaust billowed around it. Sourpuss staggered out coughing.

"Quick," he wheezed, "Drag it out of the van." His personal cloud, which had been hiding from the exhaust fumes, peeked out of the door, waited for the fumes to clear then scooted back into position over the duck's head. It began to leak a black sooty drizzle.

Whinjer and Whiner scrambled into the back of the van and, with the help of some really pongy neeps, dragged what looked like a large upturned saucer with short bandy legs out onto the road.

Sourpuss, streaks of sooty water running down his face, kicked the strange contraption with his webbed feet.

"Wake up, you lazy cowpat. Get over into the middle of the road, now. Quickly. They'll be here in a moment."

"Wot, roundabout 'ere?" queried the cowpat thing.

"That's your name innit?" growled Horace Hogsnout. "So go and earn your breakfast."

"Breakfats!" snuffled the roundabout. "Chance'd be a nife ting." Roundabouts, as you may not know, have problems speaking as few people ever listen to them. "If I hadn't squeeshed a douple of doozy neeps I wouldn't have eaten a…"

"Shaddup and get moving," snarled Sourpuss. He leapt in the air as his cloud fired a warning bolt of lightning at his head.

Grumbling, the roundabout lifted itself ponderously onto its stubby legs and trundled into the road.

"Roundabout 'ere?" he called.

"That'll do, cowpat," sneered Gofast as he fixed a Diversion sign into a hole on the top of the roundabout. "With luck they'll run over you really hard."

"Who nods inimies with freds lik you lot," muttered Roundabout 'ere.

The Grabbers scrambled back into the UWV, falling head over heels in their hurry. Within minutes the road was clear again as the UWV disappeared down the side road down which the Diversion directed traffic, to set up their ambush.

Overhead, Hurricane had seen the whole thing.

"Dashed unsporting what!" he muttered to himself. "I must warn the others." Suddenly a huge rush of air tipped him into a crazy spin. He hurtled towards the ground only just managing to pull out in time.

"Caradoc!" he shouted, looking around desperately. "I do wish you wouldn't do that. Just give me a little more airspace will you?"

Caradoc made himself visible. " Sorry boyo, just a mite excited you see. I'm nearly home again."

"Yes, well that's as maybe," spluttered Hurricane. "But did you see what those Ghastly Grabbers have planned?"

"Too right. I'll warn our lot," said Caradoc.

"Okay," responded Hurricane. "I'll go and keep an eye on the Grabbers."

Caradoc, already out of earshot (although his ears were not very big anyway), landed slap on the roundabout.

"Ooof!" exclaimed Roundabout 'ere. "Crikey mate, you're some weight."

"Well, well," mused the invisible Caradoc, "a rhyming roundabout. Whatever will they think of next."

Suddenly the Thumps appeared around the bend. They were travelling fast. Quickly Caradoc raised himself to his full height and held out his hand to stop them. Mr Thump didn't see him, mainly because Caradoc had forgotten to materialise but also because he was staring at the strange antics of the roundabout as it tried to shrug off the invisible dragon.

Crash! The front wing of the car buckled against Caradoc's invisible tail. The car and caravan scrunched to a halt by the roadside.

Everybody tumbled out to see what had happened. Caradoc, now in full view, limped over to the verge hanging his head. Trying not to look at any of the others he concentrated on readjusting his scales.

Young Kit took one look at the damage. "I think we need some help here," he said, flipping open his mobile and dialling his brother's number.

Thud walked over to the roundabout. It didn't look like a normal roundabout. He kicked it.

"Wud you mind ver much be not that doing," it pleaded. "What with Duckbilled Sourpuss's, neeps and dragons, I hink I've hid quote nufs for todday thanking you. I have desded to saty here." And with that, it drew in its legs and went to sleep. And, as far as I know, it is still there!

CHAPTER ELEVEN

Satchmo the Irrit joins the hunt

Very soon, the Thumps saw a van with a flashing yellow light approaching.

"You the ones called St C?" queried the driver.

Youg Kit explained the situation and, in a very short space of time, the wing had been straightened and they were on their way.

"I must say, that was remarkably quick service," said Mr Thump.

"Lucky you had me with you," replied Young Kit. "Otherwise you wouldn't have known how St Christopher can help you with any roadside problem – not just losing your licence from getting flashed."

"Yes, well I still don't see that worrying me," replied Mr Thump, smiling contentedly to himself.

No further mention was made of the talking roundabout. There was an unspoken agreement that it was best forgotten.

Slip had spotted a road sign with directions to the castle. "We're here, more or less. I suppose it must be about time for Gruntfettle to do his stuff." Her bored tone concealed a growing interest in their quest. Still, it would have been uncool to admit it.

Minnie placed the magic chart over the atlas. "Oh my goodness. It says here that… **'Your grunnock should now be getting quite warm. Fettle it gently so that it doesn't cause damage. Then find the quickest route to the town best approached on a cock horse. Approximately 15 miles south, as the crow flies is a timber store not far from Blenheim Palace. You need the middle letter.'**" She looked up. "Are you getting warm Mr Grunnock?"

"As a matter of fact I am a bit, O Beauteous One." Minnie Thump blushed crimson. "Hey, HH," called the Great Grunnock behind him, "Chuck over my fettling stick if it's finished breakfast will you old chum." He beamed down into the car. "Nothing like a good fettle to cool the blood," he said.

"No, I suppose there isn't," said a perplexed Mr Thump.

The top of the car bowed and creaked alarmingly as the Huge Haggis appeared at the sun-roof. "Fettling's still eating," he said. "Why not use this irrit!" He tossed the grunnock a small, many-legged, suckered and armed creature. Mr Thump glanced up as GG fettled away, humming quietly to himself. From what he could see, it looked a tad like a cross between grooming and toe-wrestling – but not really much like either. "Looks soothing, anyway. Must make a note to try that myself," he mused as he accelerated away.

Some miles behind, Sourpuss scratched his bald, lightning-scarred head. "Drat! They must have driven straight on. Okay, Gofast, let's put some rubber on the road."

Genghis 'Flash' Gofast grinned and licked his lips "What about the roundabout?"

"Leave it," snarled Sourpuss. "It was squashing too many neeps anyway."

Gofast wrinkled his nose. "Can't say I'm sorry about that," he retorted as he slammed his foot onto the accelerator. Tyres squealing and belching black exhaust, the UWV roared off.

Not far away, Mr Thump was sweating. He always did when talking to a policeman. Not that he was guilty or anything. Oh no. It was just that… well… policeman always made him nervous.

"Yes sir," said PC Bloodhound. He leaned through the window and peered around. "Hit's about heleven foot tall with… with… things and bits on hit, like. Reported seen proceeding hin a southerly direction hon the Hedinburgh Hexpress. Hay grunnock hi believe hit's called – hit's nomenclature, that his."

"Well hit's not… I mean, it's not in here as you can see," laughed Mr Thump nervously.

"Mmmm. Not obviously, no, I will allow you that sir… owhever," PC Bloodhound sniffed noisily, "there his hay strange heffluvium happarent hin the hatmosphere hin 'ere, hisn't there?"

"That'll be Crunch," piped Slip, smiling at the policeman. To confirm the point Crunch let out a long, thunderous and very pungent fart.

"Aagh!" gagged PC Bloodhound as he jerked backwards. His cap hit the roof and his tie snagged in the window. "Go hon," he gasped, flapping a hand frantically. "You'd best be movin' hon sir. Please!" His face began to turn a ripe purple colour as he struggled to unsnag his tie. Suddenly, with a ripping sound, he broke free and staggered backwards across the road, still gesturing for them to go. Behind, in the caravan, the Great Grunnock and the others crouched low on the floor … not easy if you are eleven foot tall and are enclosed in a small space with a dragon – however invisible it may be!

As they pulled away, Mr Thump breathed a huge sigh of relief.

Behind him Satchmo the Irrit sat on the rear window-sill. He was grinning and waving the tattered remains of PC Bloodhound's tie from one of his arms.

"Neat that," he said. "Even if I do say so myself."

CHAPTER TWELVE

Mr Thump in trouble

S o what else do irrits do?" enquired Slip as Satchmo clambered down and sat on Crunch's lap.

"Cor, bit strong here, isn't it?" grinned the irrit. "What do irrits do? Why, we irritate. That's what. Personally, I am a fully qualified Zipologist First Class with Whistles, Bells and Knobs On. Satchmo's the name."

Slip looked puzzled. She could see no sign of whistles, bells or knobs.

"You know," explained Satchmo. "When you're trying to pull up a zip and it sticks… then suddenly whizzes up and you smack yourself in the face?" He chortled gleefully. "That's my speciality. Or, when a door jams. You keep tugging at it. Suddenly it flies open and flattens your nose." He rolled off Crunch's lap onto the seat giggling merrily. Tears of laughter filled his eyes. "Ah, that's a brill one that. Really gets me going."

"Well you just keep your fingers and suckers and what-have-you's to yourself please Mr Irrit," said Mr Thump sternly. "We've got enough trouble as it is without you adding to it.

Satchmo made sure the driver couldn't see his "don't-get-your-knickers-in-a-twist" expression and gave Slip a broad wink.

A while later, Mr Thump roused the attention of his passengers. "Now, everyone keep your eyes skinned. We must be getting close to where we're supposed to be."

Satchmo grinned at Thud and Slip. Clambering down onto the floor he disappeared under the driving seat.

"Look at that sign post," exclaimed Thud. "Isn't that the place we want?"

"Well done son," beamed his Dad. "Very clever. Okay Minnie, where to now?"

PC 'Sniffer' Bloodhound

"Aren't we going a little fast dear?" enquired his wife nervously.

"Oh, sorry." Mr Thump frowned. The car was still picking up speed. He dabbed the brakes. It made no difference. Smoothly, the car accelerated up to 45 mph.

They shot past a sign with a camera on.

"Dad, be careful. We'll get flashed!" Thud shouted from the back.

"I can't stop it," came the anguished retort. "The accelerator seems to be stuck."

Suddenly there was a blinding flash.

"Oh my goodness. What was that?" said Minnie.

Mr Thump gritted his teeth and held onto the steering wheel. They were now doing 50 mph.

"That's three." Said Young Kit. "I'd slow down if I was you."

"Three what?" asked Mr Thump through gritted teeth. Frantically he tried to lever the accelerator back with his foot.

"Points on your licence of course. Mind you, if you were a Friend of St Christopher you wouldn't feel quite so worried."

Flash!

"Oh no, not another one," groaned Young Kit. "That's bad. One more and even big Bro won't be able to help you."

Suddenly the accelerator came free. The car slowed rapidly. Pulling in to the next lay-by Mr Thump collapsed back into his seat, sweat pouring down his face.

"I don't know what happened then," he said. "I couldn't shift the accelerator at all. It was jammed."

Satchmo crawled out from under the driver's seat and climbed back onto Crunch's lap. He was grinning from ear to ear.

"You didn't…" gasped Slip.

"Who me?" his eyes opened in wide-eyed innocence. "Would I do that?"

Satchmo the Irrit. Handle with caution

Slip looked at him in a calculating fashion. "Not funny, Satchmo," she said, finally. "You could have had us off the road … maybe worse."

"But it's what irrits are for," protested Satchmo. "No harm done, anyway – except to your Dad's blood pressure maybe," he grinned nervously.

Kit, had overheard the irrit. "Two speeding fines in as many minutes isn't exactly no harm done," he accused. "I suggest you apologise to Mr Thump right now, and you'd better convince him whose side you're really on. Otherwise you'll be out on your ear."

In the event, with the children pleading for him, Satchmo was allowed to stay. Mr Thump was enormously relieved to learn that there was nothing wrong with the car after all. But getting flashed twice for speeding – even though it hadn't been his fault – had shaken him.

"If you want Big Bro to ease your mind you'd better call him now," Kit suggested. You're up to six points already. Three more and you haven't a hope."

"Nine!" exclaimed Dad. "I can't possibly…." His voice trailed away as he realised how quickly things had suddenly changed.

"Okay," he said. "Better be safe than sorry. What do I do?"

"You can send off the form in the back of my 'Hunt the Grunnock' book Dad," said Thud.

"Or you can just call St Christopher directly," said Young Kit proffering his mobile.

Minutes later, Mr Thump breathed a sigh of relief. He was covered. "That was quick and simple," he remarked to Young Kit. "Your brother St Christopher certainly does look after travellers."

"I have a feeling we're going to need him quite a bit before we get to this treasure," Kit answered. "We've a lot of miles to cover."

Mr Thump moved carefully back onto the road. "Let's see if we can get to the next clue without any further problems."

"Turn left here, dear," said Minnie who had Gruntfettle's chart open on her lap. "We have to … **'pass through the city where Lady Godiva rode bareback (and bare everything else) to another city where Robin Hood's arch enemy lived. Steal its third letter and keep it safe.'**"

In the caravan behind, Wee Angus looked worriedly out of the back window. He felt quite sick. "Anyone smell neeps?" he asked. The others nodded. "Uh oh, I think we're in trouble," he said.

CHAPTER THIRTEEN

Thud learns how to Og a Neep

How are you doing, cousin?" the Great Grunnock enquired of the Huge Haggis. "'Cos you're looking pretty green." "You seem to have gone a strange colour yourself, Grun," HH replied.

In fact all of them in the caravan were rapidly turning a very sickly shade of green.

"We've got to stop," gasped Wee Angus "Otherwise we'll all be done for. Crikey, look at old Caradoc!"

The dragon was strobing on and off like a kaleidoscope of disco lights.

Drone the Haggipiper moaned mournfully in a corner and even the Haggiflyer, normally the bounciest of them all, was curled up holding his stomach.

"There's definitely a neep hidden somewhere," said Wee Angus, "and we're going to have to find it quickly."

Frantically he waved out of the caravan's window. Mr Thump, seeing the commotion in his mirror, pulled into the next service station.

As the car came to a halt, the occupants of the caravan tumbled out. They lay on the concrete gulping in lungfuls of air. Gradually their faces turned back from green to blue to tartan (in Drone's case) to healthy pink – all except for the GG, of course, who returned to his normal but unusual colour.

"Ne..ne....neep," croaked Wee Angus pointing at the caravan. Satchmo the irrit crawled underneath and soon reappeared dragging a scowling neep behind him. The pong was truly terrible.

"Yikes! It smells even worse than Crunch after he's had beans for tea," gagged Thud, holding his nose.

Grimacing, Mr Thump picked it up in his fingers and carried it at arm's-length, squirming and spitting angrily, towards the nearest litter bin. He slammed down the lid.

"My guess is that we picked it up off that talking roundabout," said Wee Angus thoughtfully. "I can't sense any more around."

"Yes, but it won't be the last. We're going to have to find some way of neutralising them," said HH, "or we'll be in serious trouble."

Just then, Slip pointed excitedly to the back door of the Little Chef at the side of the car park. "Look," she called, "What on earth are those things?"

They followed her gaze to where a dozen squirming thumb-sized creatures were heading through the hedge. They looked like nothing so much as outsize multicoloured furry caterpillars.

"Well, I'll be a toasted cheese sandwich with crispy bacon and just a teensy-weensy bit of ketchup on the side …only to taste of course… them's ogs or I'll be grunnocked," exclaimed the Huge Haggis.

"I don't know whether you intended that last remark as a compliment," rumbled the GG. "But you're right about them being ogs. I think we've found our neep-neutralisers, gang. Come on, after them before they get away!"

Dodging between the parked cars, the whole group tracked the strange, furry creatures. On the other side of the hedge that marked the boundary of the car-park they found themselves in a large field. It was full of row upon row of small neatly trimmed trees. From the branches, clusters of fully grown ogs swung gently in the breeze.

"Just hold it there pardners. This is private property. I can get peeved mighty quickly at trespassers. So state your business afore I fill you full of ogs."

Facing them was a large haggis wearing a stetson. He had two guns slung low on his hips and his gunbelt was full of squirming ogs.

Rapidly, the Huge Haggis explained their problem.

"Reckon you've found the right person," drawled the new haggis. "Hank McHaggis is the name, from the Texas clan. Ancestors stowed away on the first whisky shipment from Scotland. Only a few made it all the way and settled there. Fastest og shooter west of the Alamo, that's me."

"So what's an American haggis doing in England, Mr Hank?" enquired Wee Angus politely.

"Finest og-farming country in the world. Started my own

Hank McHaggis, fastest og-shooter in the world

business as you can see. Premium-quality critters." So saying, Hank pulled out one of his two very wide-barrelled guns, loaded it with giggling ogs and let fly at a neep target in the trees. Spinning rapidly, their bright fur trailing in the slipstream, the ogs whistled through the air … actually, a couple sang the first bars of 'Fly me to the Moon', but the remainder just whistled. Unerringly, all of them hit the target with a resounding squelch. They slithered to the ground and crawled quickly back to Hank chattering excitedly among themselves.

Thud was examining the branches full of ogs. "So ogs grow on trees, do they?"

"Nope. Don't you recognise a farklefruit tree when you see it, son?"

"Oh, they live on farklefruit, then?"

"Nope. Use the farklefruit rind to comb their fur."

"Comb their fur? So as to look neat?"

"Nope. To put at a left-hand twist in it."

"A twist in their fur?"

Hank looked at him. "Guess you don't know much about ogs, do you? The twist is so they spin in the air when you shoot 'em. Makes 'em more accurate. Here, you want to try?"

For the next half an hour Thud happily fired ogs at neep targets until the ogs were so exhausted they refused to be loaded any more. In the meantime, the others accepted Hank's generous offer to load the caravan with enough supplies of ogs to defeat an army of neeps.

"Reckon I'll join forces with you, if you've no objection," he suggested. "The farm can take care of itself for a few days."

The others greeted the notion with enthusiasm.

After a much needed meal at the Little Chef they drove out of the service station, heading north. They soon found the clue they were seeking and, on Minnie's instructions, turned east.

"What are we looking for?" asked Slip, who was now beginning to get into the whole treasure hunt scene.

"We have to **'drive east to find the town in the west where tea was wasted,'**" her mother replied. "It also says … **'Americans who hail from here may want to slip red socks on their grunnock before fettling it! We need to keep one of the letters repeated in the name.'** Hmmm, maybe Hank can help with this clue."

As they drove off, the UWV slipped out of a side road and slotted unnoticed into the traffic behind them.

CHAPTER FOURTEEN

Bookworm Knowitall solves the problem.

It was beginning to get dark as the Thumps headed east. "We'll have to find somewhere to spend the night soon," said Mr Thump. Thud couldn't stop yawning. Slip and Crunch were already asleep in the back.

In the caravan, Drone's snores were deafening. Hurricane grabbed some sleepy ogs and stuffed them into the haggipiper's pipes. A blissful silence descended! Caradoc glanced out of the back window. He frowned.

"See something?" queried Wee Angus.

Caradoc looked again. "Can't be sure, but I thought I saw the Ghastly Grunnock Grabbers' van in the distance." The others clambered up beside him and peered back down the road. They couldn't see anything.

"Oh, well. Just nerves I suppose," mused the dragon.

"More likely too many helpings of Welsh rarebit," muttered Drone to Wee Angus.

Fortunately, Caradoc didn't hear him. "I'll just grab some shut-eye," he said, closed one eye and promptly disappeared.

A few minutes later they were all jolted awake by the sound of the engine spluttering and coughing. Mr Thump could do nothing as the car swerved off the road and crunched into a signpost. The engine gave a final hiccup, then died. "Oh Grunnocks!" he exclaimed angrily. "What on earth caused that? I couldn't stop it happening." He walked back to the caravan and poked his head inside. "Any of you lot any good with engines?"

They shook their heads sleepily.

"Could be another job for St Christopher," yawned Young Kit as he climbed out of the car. "We'll have to ask him. Would you like to use my phone?" He held out his mobile. "Just call 08081 624046."

Mr Thump dialled, got through to St Christopher and explained the situation. His face broke into a relieved smile. "Okay everyone. As it wasn't my fault he says he can help us."

ᴥ ᷟᨓ ᷠ ⚲ ᷠ ᨓ ᴥ

Half a mile behind, the Grabbers UWV coasted silently to a halt under the shadow of a large oak tree.

"Let's go and grab the map now," Gofast suggested eagerly.

"And spit a few haggises while we're at it," growled Hogsnout.

"Nah," replied Sourpuss. "There are too many of them. We'll wait till dark before we move in. They're bound to be stuck here all night."

But shortly afterwards a breakdown van, yellow light flashing urgently, roared past them and screeched to a stop by the Thump's car.

"Stuck all night, you say?" drawled Gofast, his voice dripping with sarcasm.

Sourpuss snarled… then yelped as a mini–thunderbolt from his personal cloud zapped him. Steam jetted from his ears and nostrils.

Minnie Thump, on the other hand, was delighted to see the breakdown van. "That was quick," she said.

"St. Chris uses a huge network of local garages," explained Kit. "So, wherever you break down, there's always someone ready to help … someone or something," he amended, as he caught sight of the breakdown truck driver.

A strange wormlike creature clambered down from the cab. Actually, it wasn't worm*like*, it *was* a worm – but huge. It was wearing a mortarboard on its head, gold–rimmed spectacles and a black teacher's gown. It was carrying a large service manual under an arm and balanced upright on a knot in its tail.

"Bookworm Knowitall at your service Ladies and Gentlemen and…" he paused and studied the assembled group over the top of his spectacles, "…and other things." His voice trailed off in surprise. "How very interesting. I wonder what classification you are?" he mused, examining the Great Grunnock closely. He started to flick through his manual.

"No time for that, Bookworm – we need to get going again, like now." Young Kit grabbed hold of Bookworm's elbow and hustled him round to the front of the car.

Bookworm lifted the bonnet, leaned over and and peered inside. His mortarboard slipped down over his eyes. "Dark in here. Anyone got a torch?"

Bookworm Knowitall, skilled mechanic
and night-school teacher

Kit reached out and removed the offending headgear.

"Ah, right, thank you," said Knowitall. "Sorry about that. The call from the boss came through just as I was about to go out to teach my evening class: 'Og Breeding for Fun and Profit'." He caught the expression on Mr Thud's face. "Still, I'm sure you don't want to hear about that now," he said briskly. "Let's see what the problem is."

The others watched in amazement as, with a twist of his boneless body, he propelled his head deep into the engine.

"Aha, thought so…well 'pon my word. Mmmmmmmm…might need to… should be able… with a little tweak there…." Bookworm jerked hard at something. Triumphantly he held up the cause of the problem. In his hand was a very small irrit.

"Muncho," called Satchmo in delight "What are you doing here?" The small irrit looked down. "Oh, hi Uncle Satchmo. I was tidying up some of those electrical wires in there. Terrible mess they were in."

"Well done lad. Trained by one of the best… me!" Satchmo beamed with pride until he saw the angry faces staring at him. He gulped. "Er, possibly not the best time for a demo, though."

"Well, Mr Irrit, this is what I am trained to do," said Bookworm sternly. Holding Muncho in one hand he grabbed Satchmo in the other. Expertly he twined them around the wires in the engine and touched them together. There was a loud fizzing sound, blue sparks flew between the two irrits who shrieked in agony and suddenly the car roared back into life. "Follow me to the garage," called Bookworm as he climbed back into his truck, chortling to himself. "Those pesky irrits will hold for a few miles until I can make a permanent repair."

CHAPTER FIFTEEN

The first great battle

The Thumps pulled into a garage a few miles down the road, much to the relief of two very chastened and singed irrits! As the garage doors closed behind the car, the Grunnock Grabbers shot past along the road hotly pursued by PC Bloodhound and Sergeant Mole. Gofast had deliberately triggered more flashes as he followed the Thumps, adding to his personal tally.

Young Kit was talking to the garage proprietor: a weird-looking character who could best be described as a cross between a large octopus and a small elephant. The Thumps had already met so many strange creatures in the past few hours that none of them batted an eyelid when faced with this latest one.

With so many tentacles, Ollyphant (for that was his name) reconnected the electrics in no time. Satchmo, still smouldering and emitting occasional sparks, was very relieved. He didn't try to meet anybody's eye and slunk away in disgrace along with Muncho.

"Right. There you go, chaps," boomed Ollyphant. He looked round at the strange gathering. "Carrying some oddball characters here," he trumpeted with laughter.

Ollyphant, the strangest motor mechanic you ever saw

"Think I'll join the party if that's okay with you. Looks like fun and you might need me again – you never know!" So saying he climbed aboard the caravan as Major Thump drove out of the garage. It wasn't long before they came to a crossroads. The headlights lit up a large sign.

Slip pointed. "That must be the place we're looking for. I remember, we did the bit about the wasted tea in History last term. And there's one letter that's repeated, as it said in the clue."

"You're right," exclaimed his Dad, "But we'd better not go straight on. Look!"

Some distance ahead through the gloom they could just make out the Grunnock Grabbers' van, black smoke belching from the exhaust. Behind them a blue flashing light showed that Bloodhound and Mole had not lost the scent.

"Can't we go right?" queried Slip. "It looks clear that way."

Minnie placed the magic map over the road atlas again. "Left would be better," she said. "Here's what it says … **'Travel north to find the Viking city where the A19 crosses the A64. Take the A166 to the place where Harold beat Harold and Chelsea fans cheer. Ha! Fettled you now. The last letter is the one you want to keep.'"**

Filled with renewed confidence after seeing the Grabbers disappear in the wrong direction, they turned onto the main road and headed north.

A few minutes later and several miles away, PC Bloodhound skidded to a halt. His windscreen wipers screeched slowly against the black gunk that spewed out of the Grunnock Grabbers' exhaust.

"Double drat!" exclaimed Sergeant Mole. "No windscreen wash in the reservoir and we can't see a thing through this muck. We're losing them."

While PC Bloodhound climbed out and cleaned the windscreen as best he could with the remains of his tie, his sergeant worked out what to do next.

"Tell you what," he said. "Let's head back to the crossroads and follow that crowd with the caravan. The lot we're chasing seem to be chasing them so we'll catch them when they meet up."

"Okay, boss." He put the car in gear and executed a neat three-point turn.

Up ahead, Gofast spotted the move in his rear-view mirror. "Hey Duck, they've turned back. We're okay."

Sourpuss grunted as studied the road map.

"Good. Now, follow this route and we can get ahead of those blasted Thumps and set up an ambush. We must get hold of that magic chart!"

With a grinding of gears the UWV roared off into the night.

It was dawn when the Thumps finally found the answer to the clue.

"Hey, there's a sign says it's an old battlefield," said Thud. They had all piled out onto the roadside and were stretching their legs.

Suddenly, Hurricane, who had gone up for a morning recce, came barrelling out of the sky.

"Enemy attack," he shouted. "The Grabbers and neeps are just over the rise. And they're headed this way!"

The warning was nearly too late as a platoon of neeps came charging over the hill towards them uttering their shrill war cry of 'Neep…Neep…Neep!'

"Quick, circle the wagons," shouted Hank McHaggis. Mr Thump just looked at him with raised eyebrows.

Hank reconsidered. "Okay, Plan B. Everyone tool up!" He dashed back to the caravan and rapidly handed out ogshooters and bandoliers of excited ogs. He was just in time. Seconds later battle was joined.

The fight was fierce and no quarter given. Again and again the neeps attacked. Their revolting smell threatening to asphyxiate the gallant band, particularly the haggises who were most affected. But the grunnock gang and Thump family kept firing og after og into their attackers, breaking the advancing wave again and again.

Drone bounced up and down on the roof of the caravan exhorting his friends with stirring Scottish battle tunes, while Hurricane dropped og bombs with devastating effect. Caradoc kept appearing behind the enemy line, toasting their rear-ends with flame, then loosing off a few deadly shots before disappearing again. Slip had managed to adapt some knicker-elastic into a remarkably effective catapult, and one of her well-aimed ogs sent Gofast's shades spinning.

Hold your nose! Here come the neeps…

Wielding his wicked cleaver, Hogsnout led a final desperate charge. Olly's tentacles became a blur as he whipped og-grenades at the murderous Haggis Hacker and his troops. Hogsnout's snarl of rage became a scream of pain when a spinning og caught him square on his nose.

Soon it was all over and the neeps were totally smothered. The Grabbers and their battered troops retreated to the UWV, the little black cloud firing continuous flashes of lightning onto the singed head of the defeated Sourpuss. Thunder rumbled around his head. Exhausted by their efforts, the victorious grunnock gang just watched them go.

Hank rounded up the ogs who were chanting their ancient victory songs and outdoing each other recounting their brave deeds. Their fur was in a terrible state, but Hank handed out farklefruit-rind combs and the ogs settled down contentedly to some serious grooming.

"Kettle's boiling," announced Minnie.

Tired but victorious, everyone clambered back into the caravan for a victory breakfast of muffins and marmalade.

... but here come the ogs to clobber them

CHAPTER SIXTEEN

Nabbed!

Sticky but satisfied, the exhausted grunnock gang settled down for a victory snooze. It was crowded but quite cosy really. Thud, Slip and Crunch curled up in the warm fur of the Great Grunnock. Caradoc kept guard across the doorway.

Satchmo amused himself by tying double knots in all the shoelaces he could find. Soon they were sound asleep. The caravan vibrated to the rhythm of gentle snores.

Much later, a shadowy shape crept up to the Thumps' car. Caradoc, who had fallen asleep on guard duty, never heard a thing. The figure rummaged under the engine for a few moments and then disappeared into the darkness.

෴ ฅ๓ ฦ ﾞ ฦ ฅ๓ ෴

In a nearby village Genghis Gofast was also creeping about. This time it was Bloodhound and Mole who were the target. The policemen were enjoying forty winks in the cells inside the local police station. Sneaking inside Gofast picked up their neatly folded uniforms then climbed into their car. He released the handbrake. Silently the car rolled down the hill. When he was out of earshot Genghis let out a wild whoop and, starting the engine, roared off into the night.

෴ ฅ๓ ฦ ﾞ ฦ ฅ๓ ෴

A few hours later, Mr Thump and the grunnock gang were driving west along the motorway. They were stiff and sore after the battle.

"We're definitely heading the right way," said Minnie. "It says … **'Travel west to catch a ferry to an island where the cats have no tails and the people can't fall over (check the motto). When you get there, look for an archangel and take the first or last letter of his church.'"**

Mr Thump was uneasy. He glanced in his rear view mirror again. The Grabbers van was behind them again. And behind it was a police car. He didn't say a word to the others. Strange though…the UWV was just keeping pace, following them a few hundred metres behind.

They were just starting down a steep hill when disaster struck. As Mr Thump dabbed the brakes there was a loud *Kerboooing*! The brake pedal hit the floor.

"Hold on everybody. The brakes have failed."

Everyone looked at Satchmo who made frantic 'No No No, not me!' gestures and glared at Muncho who made equally frantic 'Nor me neither, honest!' gestures.

Quickly the car gathered speed, the caravan swaying along behind. Faster and faster they went. Mr Thump wrestled with the wheel, sweat pouring from his brow. By some miracle he managed to keep the car on the road until, as the carriageway levelled and started to rise again, the car slowed enough to pull over to the side.

Shaking and drenched in sweat, they collapsed in relief.

But they relaxed too soon.

The police car that Mr Thump had seen earlier, screeched to a halt in front of them. In his mirror he saw the Grabbers' UWV coast to a halt behind. They were trapped!

Winjer and Whiner, dressed in ill-fitting police uniforms, sauntered up to the car.

"Right you lot. You was definitely speeding back there then and so we's arresting you all." They wrenched open the car doors. "Outside. Now. All of you."

"You're not real police," exclaimed Thud.

"Quiet son," whispered his Dad. "Best do what they say for the moment."

As the Thump family, Young Kit and Satchmo the Irrit clambered shakily on to the verge they saw Sourpuss standing triumphantly at the door of the caravan. Genghis stood behind him holding a key. Hammering came from inside the caravan. Their friends were locked in! Wee Angus and the others stared helplessly out the windows.

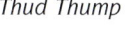

Thud Thump

Sourpuss waddled up to Mr Thump, an evil grin on his beak.

"I'll have the chart if you please," he rasped. "Now – or you'll be sorry!"

Minnie clutched the chart to her bosom while Mr Thump drew himself up to his full height. He towered over the duck. "Mind the cloud Dad," murmured Thud nervously.

His father swayed to one side.

"Never!" he said forcefully.

Sourpuss shrugged. "Suit yourself." He turned. "Oi, Genghis. Take the littlest kid and feed him to the neeps."

"No!" Minnie shouted in horror "You wouldn't dare, you mangy chicken." She swung her handbag with all her might. It caught Sourpuss on the end of his duckbill and sent him tumbling into the ditch at the side of the road. He scrambled out, screaming with anger, the cloud firing hailstones and lightning at him like a machine gun.

"It's alright, Missus," said Satchmo, "You can let him have it."

"That's just what she's done," said Thud proudly.

Satchmo grinned. "No. I mean the chart. It doesn't matter anyway. It's run out. Look. It says we have to find the next clue and then we will get the second part of the map. And we know where we're going don't we?" They all nodded and looked at the irate duck who snatched the chart from Minnie, glanced at it then threw it back at her.

"Right," snarled Sourpuss. "In that case we'll go there together. Get in, the lot of you! Gofast, you drive them. Whinjer, you go with them too. Whiner you drive our van and take him with you," he pointed at Thud.

"Now, take us to the next clue – and no tricks!"

Clambering in, they left the police car by the side of the road and drove off westwards.

Sergeant "Digger" Mole

CHAPTER SEVENTEEN

Over the briny

PC Bloodhound and Sergeant Mole were not happy policemen. It had taken them hours to find their car and trying to explain to Chief Inspector Dent how they had lost it was a humiliating experience. Now, as they drove onto the ferry in pursuit of the Ghastly Grunnock Grabbers and their UWV, they were in an ugly mood.

"You sure they caught this ferry?" snarled Mole.

"Absolutely," replied Bloodhound through gritted teeth. "I checked with a cousin of mine. He's in the Force on the Island. They landed this morning. He said that the van nearly asphyxiated him as it drove down the ramp." He looked at Mole who was turning a delicate shade of green. "You all right?"

"'Course I am. Just don't like the sea much, that's all. Pass me those sea-sick pills."

"But we're still tied to the jetty!"

"I don't care. It's rocking like a roller coaster. Just give me the pills."

Bloodhound shrugged and passed him the pills. Then he reached down and opened a large pack of sandwiches he had bought at the ticket office. A strong smell of hot bacon filled the air.

"Fancy a bacon sarny, Sarge?" he enquired.

But Sergeant Mole was nowhere to be seen – or, rather, only the bottom half could be seen. His top half was doubled over the ship's rail.

The duckbilled Sourpuss couldn't understand what had happened. One minute he had everything under control. On the way over on the ferry he had told Horace Hogsnout to stay in the caravan with a pocketful of neeps to keep the haggises subdued, while he and Gofast kept an eye on the others in the car.

Suddenly it had all gone wrong. They had landed at the capital of the Island amid a cacophony of roaring motor bikes. It appeared that some kind of festival was happening. Something to do with tea he thought. Or two teas maybe? At least, that's what it sounded like.

Gofast had been getting hyped up all the way over but, when he heard the bikes he had gone bananas. Leaping from the car he had jumped on to a bike and roared of down the road. Sourpuss had leapt out to stop him. All he got for his trouble was tyre-tracks etched neatly across his warty webbed feet. While he was hopping up and down in agony, Mr Thump had grabbed the wheel and driven off. Thud had slipped out of the back of the UWV and into his Dad's car and, back in the caravan, Caradoc and the haggises had managed to overpower Hogsnout. They had opened a window and now they were hurling furious neeps into the road.

It was total chaos.

As the car rocketed along the road, the caravan swayed behind. The haggises, released from the stupefying smell of neep, finally managed to push Hogsnout and Whinjer out of the back. They bounced and rolled into the ditch with the last neep.

All together once again, the Thumps and friends roared off towards the west of the Island where they thought the next clue was.

Some way behind them Whiner trundled slowly along in the UWV picking up some very angry and dishevelled neeps and the other Grunnock Grabbers – except Gofast of course. He was just starting his second lap of the racecourse having broken the lap record, with fourteen police bikes frantically trying to catch him.

The Thumps had stopped opposite the site of the clue.

"That's the answer all right," said Minnie, "but where do we find the next map?"

"You already have it," piped up Satchmo, grinning broadly.

"But, you said …"

"I know. I told a bit of a porky, and Sourpuss swallowed it. But …" he clambered onto Minnie's lap, "all we have to do is… turn it over!"

And there was the next clue sharp and clear.

"Cross back to the mainland. Head north to Stranraer. From there head north again. The A77 will take you to a town where the Scottish 'yes' has an 'e' removed, replaced by an 'aarr' which you need. Don't allow the grunnock to distract you because you are now getting quite warm."

"But that means another sea crossing!" moaned Satchmo, going green.

"You really are quite bright, aren't you," complimented Mr Thump. "But," he added quickly as the irrit climbed onto his knee, "you can still keep your hands, suckers and things off the car! And that goes for Junior as well."

Satchmo's face dropped and he clambered into the back and sulked on Slip's lap.

"Right, we'd better head back to the ferry."

"You'll have to go right round the racetrack I think," said Young Kit. "These bikes are everywhere and they all seem to be going in the same direction. Mad Sunday I believe they call it. The whole Island becomes one way."

"Crazee!" exclaimed Thud as another huge mass of bikes roared past. "Let's go, Dad."

Rather gingerly, Mr Thump manoeuvred the car and caravan out into the thundering traffic. They were immediately surrounded by a phalanx of bikes. Some miles behind, the Grabbers' white van was in a similar situation.

An hour later, deafened by the earsplitting noise, they trundled back down onto the ferry. The UWV arrived some time later, coasting silently down the ramp. As the ferry started to pull away from the dock, Gofast appeared at full speed followed by all the police motorcyclists on the Island. Twisting the throttle fully open, he took off from the end of the ramp, sailed across the widening gap, and landed with an earsplitting squeal of brakes on the deck. Grinning from ear to ear he climbed off the bike and into the waiting arms of Sergeant Mole and PC Bloodhound.

"'Ello, 'ello, 'ello," said Mole. "Hand what do we 'ave 'ere? You're coming wiv us sunshine." And they marched him off out of sight.

Sourpuss watched from behind a ventilator. "Huh. Good riddance to bad rubbish," he snarled, ducking as his personal cloud fired a bolt of lightning onto his head and then opened up with a drenching cold shower.

"One day, cloud!" yelled Sourpuss shaking a fist. "One day!"

CHAPTER EIGHTEEN

Banned!

If the Thumps had been hoping to carry on their way unhindered, they were sadly mistaken. White and shaken from a rough crossing, they found themselves stopped by police as they drove off the ferry. Their antics of the last few days had not gone unnoticed. Mole and Bloodhound had called ahead to organise a reception committee.

The only consolation was that they weren't alone. Bunched together with the Grunnock Grabbers, they were marched straight to the courthouse and paraded before the local magistrate.

Justice was swift and sharp, as the magistrate had ambitions to become a judge. He was as bald as a snooker ball and fancied himself in the wig. In fact, on that very morning he had an urgent appointment with his wig-maker who had promised him the new 'Beckham' look, so he was keen to get the sentencing over.

For 'repeated speeding offences' Genghis Gofast and Mr Thump were both disqualified from driving. Gofast was grounded for six months and poor Mr Thump one. He was aghast.

"Disqualified!" he moaned as they trooped back into the street. "I don't believe this? Me! I've always been a careful driver. It's just not fair!"

"Don't worry," Young Kit consoled him, "It's only for one month."

"One month!" he wailed. "And who will take the kids to school? Who's going to drive down to Tesco's and get the food? How can I drive to work and…"

"And how are we going to find the rest of the clues to get to my Secret Grunnock Grove?" interrupted the Great Grunnock sternly. "This is not good," he harrumphed as he stalked off towards the caravan.

"Calm down everybody." Young Kit called placatingly. "I told you my big bro always helps out his travelling friends, didn't I?" They nodded uncertainly. The Great Grunnock cocked a few ears and listened.

"Well that's fine then. Let's find someone to drive us. St C will pay for it, and we're on the road again. It's that easy. Okay?"

Looking much happier, they trooped into a convenient Little Chef for breakfast where Young Kit got on his mobile.

Half an hour later a smartly dressed young lady sauntered into the restaurant.

"Is there a Thump party in here?" she called.

Mr Thump choked on his 'Special Burger'. "Yeff. Offer here," he mumbled, spraying the table with crumbs.

"Hi there," the young lady replied. "I'm your driver, courtesy of St Christopher. Patience Driver's the name. You can call me PD." She gave the assembled party a brilliant smile.

Thud stared wide-eyed as his father stood up to meet their new acquaintance. Quickly PD was introduced to the whole gang. The Great Grunnock glowed with embarrassment (rose pink) and pleasure (bright yellow) as it was introduced. He was so overcome that he had to go back to the caravan and lie down for a bit. Which was

Patience Driver, aka PD

a pity, because it meant that a few minutes later he missed an unexpected encounter with someone he would have recognised.

PD declined the offer of a burger breakfast, remarking that, if they were to find the Grunnocks' Grove that Young Kit had told her about 'hadn't we better be getting along?'

At the mention of the Grove a hairy, hoary man dressed in baggy cycle shorts, a diver's air cylinder on his back, who had just entered the restaurant came clomping over to them.

"Excuse me," he wheezed, drawing gulps of oxygen from a tube that led to the air tank, "I couldn't help overhearing. Are you looking for the Sacred Grunnock Grove?"

"We are indeed," exclaimed Mr Thump. "Why, do you know where it is?"

A faraway glint entered the rheumy eyes of the strange man. "No, no, no idea," he said vaguely. A broad smile lit up his face. "I'm just pleased to know that my message finally got through. Name's Blowen," he said. "Colonel Blowen. You see, the thing about grunnocks is … no, on second thoughts, I don't think there's anything I can tell you that would help you." With a friendly wave, he wandered away from them and out of the restaurant.

"Strange fellow," remarked The Huge Haggis, looking after him. "What was that about a message? I don't suppose we'll ever know. Anyway, hadn't we better get moving? I don't know where Sourpuss and his gang are but I'll bet they're up to no good."

Soon they were all packed into the car and caravan ready to continue their quest. Mr Thump sat in the passenger seat while Minnie moved into the back seat with the map.

"Where to, Mrs Thump?" called PD. Minnie told her and they moved off along the A77. They hadn't gone far when they passed the Grabbers' UWV leapfrogging along the road. Sourpuss was at the wheel and it was quite obvious that he hadn't driven for a long time…if ever! It looked as if Gofast was trying to tell him what to do. Sweat poured down his face and his shades had misted over. He thought about wiping them but decided he'd rather not see exactly what the mad duck was doing. Horace Hogsnout, Whinjer and Whiner were sitting white-faced behind them, holding on tight. Sourpuss's cloud had retreated to a point several feet above the cab.

Seeing the Thumps pass him, Sourpuss pressed web to metal, determined not to lose them.

Behind the van, Mole and Bloodhound followed at a discreet distance. Both were wearing broad smiles as they watched the UWV jerking and coughing its way towards the mountains in the wake of the Thump's car.

"Just wait," grinned Mole. "One false move and we'll 'ave that duck as well. I wonder where they're heading?"

Chapter Nineteen

We all live in a UWV submarine

The Thumps had found the answer to the clue without any trouble and were now now poring over the next one. **"Find your way to the A85 and Oban,"** instructed Minnie. **"From here you must take the ferry to the beautiful island of Mull, locate the womble and remove his first letter."**

"Well, I can do the first bit," said PD, "while you lot *mull* over the rest of it." The universal groan that met her words was neither undeserved nor unexpected.

With PD driving they made quick time to Oban. The highlands of Scotland were radiant in the spring sunshine and heather covered the hillsides. In the caravan, the haggises were pointing out landmarks with excitement. Apparently they hadn't been this far west since Bonnie Prince Charlie met the Scottish clans at Glenfinnan in 1745!

The Great Grunnock had captured its fettling stick (which had been sulking in a corner as everyone seemed to have forgotten about it), and was fettling away with it behind most of its ears – humming happily to itself. If Mr Thump had been watching he would have revised his former description of fettling – not so much a cross between grooming and toe-wrestling as a cross between earwax-removal and fur-plaiting.

Every now and again the Great Grunnock poked its head out of the roof and, stretching forward peered in through the open sun-roof of the Thumps' car.

"Are we nearly there?" it beamed.

PD's smooth straight course down the road took on a distinct wobble.

"GG, do you have to sneak up on me like that?" she complained. "Can't you give me some warning?"

"Warning?" A puzzled frown appeared between three of the Grunnock's antennae. "Like this you mean?" And it let out an enormous bellow. PD nearly swerved into a rock at the side of the road.

"No, you numbskull. Not so loud."

"That was a mere whisper, lady fair," muttered the Great Grunnock and disappeared back into the caravan in a huff.

Thud and Slip convulsed into giggles in the back seat. "Can we take the Grunnock into school with us when we get back, Dad?" asked Thud. "He's well cool."

"Hey," exclaimed Slip. "Has anybody seen Satchmo recently?" They all looked around the car. Mr Thump looked worried. "If I can't see that scamp it makes me nervous," he said.

"He said something about 'giving the bill a thrill' or something like that," piped up Muncho the little irrit who was tangling Crunch's hair through Minnie's necklace. "Said I couldn't go with him 'cos it was 'serious irrit business First Class'," he pouted and carried on tangling with a ferocious intensity.

At that moment PD spotted a police car coming up fast behind her. She frowned and glanced at the speedometer. It couldn't be her they were after, she was well within the speed limit.

It wasn't. With a banshee howl of the siren, the police car drew level. The occupants, Mole and Bloodhound were white as sheets and looked terrified.

PD braked to allow the police car to pull ahead. Satchmo suddenly appeared at the open window beside Bloodhound. He leapt across to the Thump's car using his suckers to attach himself. A moment later, he clambered in through the sunroof. He was grinning widely, slapping a few arms together with satisfaction.

"That should keep them busy for a while," he chortled as the police car disappeared into the distance.

"What did you do, Irrit," demanded Mr Thump sternly.

Satchmo turned his big innocent eyes on him. "Nothing much, honest. I just tweaked his flugulerator, toggled the throttle widget and reset the grommet didger. Sorry can't translate those out of 'irrit'. Anyway, it worked didn't it? They kept on saying they ... 'didn't half fancy seeing what the old buggy could do on these great roads up here.' So I ... well, I helped them out!"

They watched as the police car, a flash of blue and white, appeared briefly in the distance before whipping around a bend and disappearing from view.

"Well I suppose they can cope," said a worried Minnie Thump. "I mean

Slip Thump, smarter than she looks

police cars always go fast like that with

their sirens wailing on the telly, don't they?"

Satchmo nodded. "It's only a temporary tweak, anyway. They'll slow down in a minute." Unnoticed, he joined Muncho in making a complete rat's nest of Crunch's hair and Minnie's necklace as she cuddled the toddler to her.

The car and caravan finally arrived in Oban in the late afternoon. The ferry for Mull was waiting and they were able to drive straight on. They clambered out and stretched their legs. The whole group wandered over to the stern rail and watched as the crew began to raise the ramp.

Suddenly they heard a horn blowing frantically. The Grabbers' UWV, smoke pouring from the exhaust was rocketing down towards them, swerving wildly across the road.

They watched as passers-by leapt for their lives. The ferrymen took no notice. They were used to latecomers trying to get on board.

"Let 'em catch the next one. They're only sassenachs, anyway," called a red-faced crewman to his mate as he locked the ramp in place – closed.

Sourpuss, desperately trying to hold the speeding van on the road, saw what was happening.

"Brakes!" he screamed at Gofast.

"That would be an excellent idea," said Gofast through gritted teeth as the end of the jetty rushed towards them. "Preferably at your earliest conveneience," he added.

"I can't reach them, imbecile!" screamed Sourpuss trying to peer through the rain and shafts of lightning that his cloud was firing at him with great excitement.

Hogsnout gaped at Sourpuss. "You drove all the way 'ere without being able to reach the brakes?"

But he was destined not to receive an answer. With a mighty roar the van soared off the end of the jetty, missed the ferry completely and crashed into the harbour in a huge welter of spray.

"Told 'em. Should ha' waited for the next y'un," shrugged the crewman. "They'll not get there in that thing," he opined, as the van sank rapidly from view. He turned his back on the frothing water and made his way to the galley 'for a brew'.

Behind them, the heads of the Grabbers popped to the surface, surrounded by sputtering neeps. They all started swimming back to the jetty. All except one.

Wee Angus looked back as the town of Oban disappeared behind the headland. Three feet above the surface of the sea, a small black cloud was zigzagging along in their wake. Every now and then it zapped off a bolt of lightning.

Chapter Twenty

Viking memories

The Isle of Mull lies in the Inner Hebrides off the west coast of Scotland. It is one of the most beautiful of all the Scottish islands. The sun bathed the trees in a warm evening light as the Thumps drove off the ferry. They were pretty certain where the clue was located, having checked their road atlas and they drove to the town that bore the name they wanted. By the time they arrived and parked outside the Mishnish Hotel, darkness had fallen. With the clue safely in their pocket, they all trooped into the bar of this famous hostelry.

Minnie and the children found a table tucked away in the corner of the snug where, as the landlord said… "if the polis canna see ye then they canna complain t' me!" Minnie took out the road atlas and laid Gruntfettle's map over it. The writing was very faint but, with the help of Thud and Slip she was able to decipher it.

"By now your grunnock should be leaping about with excitement. Calm it with song or butterscotch. Your next journey lies north on the A82 where Bill's strategic outpost welcomes you. Keep his last letter."

"Butterscotch!" exclaimed Minnie. "And just where am I supposed to find butterscotch at this time of night?"

"Well we're going to need something Mum," said Slip pointing. "It looks like the GG is already leaping with excitement. Looks to me like he's been sampling the local whisky."

On the dance floor the Great Grunnock and the Huge Haggis were engaged in what might be described as a 'Highland Fling' or possibly a 'Drunksome Reel'. Unfortunately, what they were flinging and unreeling were ogs and haggises, as they thundered about on the dance floor, urged on by the local Ceilidh band.

Drone the Haggipiper was in his element bouncing up and down on top of the paino, his skirling pipes emitting earsplitting sounds that seemed to drive the lumbering dancers into an even greater frenzy.

Haggises and ogs bounced off the walls and tables, eagerly returning to the fray in some kind of ancient war dance. Chairs crashed over, glasses smashed onto the floor and the air was wild with singing, shouting and … a strange muted trumpet sound from Ollyphant. Normally shy in a crowd, he had finally been coaxed (by the offer of a wee dram) out of his cupboard in the caravan and was swinging from the beams hanging on with a couple of tentacles.

"Enough!" shouted the landlord as the Huge Haggis skittered backwards bringing down a complete table full of glasses. At the same time, the Great Grunnock, impelled in the opposite direction, swept the bar clean with one of his appendages that seemed to have a mind of its own.

"I've never seen the like since the *Odin's Raven* Vikings hit this place in 1979."

"Aye that was a night to remember," agreed an ancient local as he fished an og out of his ale and eyed it speculatively.

"A night!" said another. "As I remember, it went on for a couple of days."

"And I'm still paying for it," muttered a distinguished white haired gentleman wearing the latest in Barbour fishing clobber, complete with coloured fishing flies stuck all over him. "It's been the same ever since," he grumbled as he headed out into the night. "Thought they were quite normal people… Dressed 'em up as Vikings, let em loose in a Viking ship and they've been the bane of my life ever since. Can't seem to get rid of them…" His voiced disappeared into the night.

"Who was that?" asked Mr Thump.

The landlord shrugged. "Can't recall his name. Came in with the Vikings back in '79 then re-appeared a couple of years ago. Apparently some of them were heading back to Norway. He stayed here to do some fishing. Keeps saying that they won't find him here and he may get some peace and quiet but…" he tapped his nose with his finger, "maybe they will, maybe they won't. Who knows."

Dad helped him pick up some of the chairs as the Grunnock and Huge Haggis, arms linked, staggered outside and meandered back to the caravan. The rest of the party followed behind. As they clambered into the car the landlord appeared in the doorway. The party was still in full swing behind him.

"Who's going to pay for this lot then?"

"Try the old Viking," called Young Kit. "He seems used to it. Tell him we won't let on where he is hiding!"

"That should do it," grinned the landlord

"Everyone aboard?" enquired PD. "Okay, let's go." And with much singing and merriment the car and caravan proceeded to the jetty at the end of the promenade and straight on to the waiting ferry, for the mainland.

Just as the ferry was about to leave, a small, disconsolate, exhausted black cloud hovered over the jetty railings. It dredged up just enough energy to fire a single petulant burst of drizzle at the sodden duck who hauled himself out of the water under the railings and collapsed on the pavement.

"Made it!" he gasped.

"Not quite, soggyfeathers," chimed a voice.

Sourpuss turned his head wearily. Satchmo the Irrit whistled as he whipped some stringy seaweed around the duck's webbed feet and the promenade railings.

"We're just off on the ferry over there. Back to the mainland. Happy hunting, duckface." With a final flourish, he tied a knot in the seaweed and scampered off to the ferry.

"That irrit has a long overdue date with Hogsnout's cleaver," snarled Sourpuss as he struggled to get up. His personal cloud dropped a little lower.

"Don't even think about it," rasped the duck. "One bolt of lightning from you and you're history!"

The cloud quivered and shunted sideways to think about it. Meteorology, fine: history, absolutely not. It coughed, fired the tiniest of sparks then pointedly turned its back on the trussed duck. The effect was rather lost as clouds look the same from front or back.

The ferry's horn echoed around the small bay as it headed away from the jetty and turned for the mainland.

"And great globs of greasy grunnocks to you too," spat Duckbilled Sourpuss angrily.

Crunch Thud

CHAPTER TWENTY ONE

Overhauled by the enemy

It was still before dawn when the Thumps rolled back onto the mainland, unaware that Horace Hogsnout, heavily disguised as a local fisherman, was sitting on a bollard watching them arrive. That was when they made their first mistake. Mr Thump looked around at the tired figures of his party. "I think we'd better let everyone get some sleep."

"Shouldn't we keep going?" PD replied. "I'm wide awake and we could get to the next clue in time for brunch."

While the others had been in the Mishnish 'partying on', PD – the driver – had very sensibly been grabbing some zeds.

Mr Thump yawned and stretched. The disguised Hogsnout sauntered past just in time to hear him say: "No, we all need a good few hours' sleep. Tell you what. Stay on the A85. Pull over when you find a suitable lay-by, please. When we've had a rest we'll have a bite then pick up the A82 north and do some sightseeing on the way. No reason why we shouldn't enjoy ourselves, now that those Ghastly Grunnock Grabbers are out of the picture."

He couldn't have been more wrong.

Round the corner, out of sight, Horace Hogsnout found Gofast pulling the last pieces of seaweed out of the engine of the UWV. It looked and smelled as if it had been at the bottom of the harbour, which of course is exactly where it had been. As Hogsnout opened the driver's door a large jellyfish sshlooped out onto his boots.

Angrily he kicked it off the jetty and glared at the tractor that had pulled the van out. It was parked a short distance away. Rescue hadn't come cheap. In a fit of pique, he crossed to the tractor, ripped off the distributor cap and tossed it in the harbour. Then he grabbed the reluctant Gofast and manhandled him up into the sodden driver's seat.

"I don't care whether you're banned from driving for life. You'll drive this thing until we get that chart!" he snarled.

Gofast curled his lip and muttered under his breath. "This heap of rust'll never work again anyway."

He turned the key.

There was a tooth-tingling grunging noise, a squeal, a splat as something very slimy slipped out of the exhaust and then a clattering roar as the engine started. Possibly the thick coating of filthy oil had protected it from the seawater.

"'Ead north," ordered Hogsnout.

"Why north?" shouted Gofast above the noise of the engine.

"Cos that's where they was 'eaded, sunbeam." He grinned evilly. "And, if I'm right, there's a perfick spot to ambush 'em. Just perfick."

Belching black smoke and backfiring like a machine gun, the van struggled up the road, clattering away on a couple of cylinders. It headed after the Thumps' caravan.

An hour later, Crunch woke up. Something had driven past sounding as if it was dragging a heap of scrap metal along the road. Through the window he saw a cloud of smoke and a single red light disappearing in the distance. A strange smell of barbecued mackerel hung in the air long after whatever it was had gone. Crunch thought about letting out a wail but dropped the idea. He was fond of his parents but when it came to cottoning on to what he was trying to tell them they were the pits. He stuck a thumb in his mouth and went back to sleep.

Morning dawned misty and with a fine Scottish drizzle blanketing the mountains. Cold and hungry, everyone struggled awake.

"Better find somewhere for breakfast, PD," yawned Mr Thump.

PD slipped the car into gear and they pulled smoothly out of the lay-by and onto the road. In a very short space of time they found a café open at Tyndrum.

Groggily they all tumbled into the warmth. The smell of frying bacon and eggs filled the room. The Huge Haggis's stomach rumbled so loudly that the rest of the diners hung onto their shaking tables. It was like a mini-earthquake.

Soon, the cook was firing out sausages, eggs, bacon, fried bread, tomatoes, beans, mushrooms and toast as fast as he could. Finally, their hunger satisfied they trooped outside again. The mist had cleared and Rannoch Moor stretched in front of them.

Mr Thump was the last to leave, a pained expression on his face.

"We'd better find these last clues soon," he murmured to Minnie as they walked to the car. "This treasure hunt is turning out to be a very expensive business!"

"Kit promised us some treasure as compensation," Minnie reminded him.

"Hmm. I'll believe it when I see it."

His mood lifted as they meandered across Rannoch Moor. The sun burned off the mist and it was turning into a 'fine and sunny' day as promised on the weather forecast. In the distance they could see the forbidding mountains of Glencoe.

"Spooky place!" exclaimed Thud.

"Is that where the Glencoe massacre was, Dad? When the Campbells attacked the McDonalds while they were asleep," asked Slip showing off her knowledge of history. Thud stuck his tongue out at her. "Know-it-all!" he muttered.

"McDonalds?" Satchmo suddenly woke up. "Food? I couldn't eat another thing."

Mr Thump laughed. "Your'e not going to either," he said. "It's probably the only place you won't find a McDonalds."

As they drove off Rannoch Moor and down into Glencoe the mountains closed in around them, overshadowing the road. It was indeed very spooky and a strange silence descended in both the car and the caravan. Near the end of the glen there was a big Visitor's Centre where the massacre had taken place. PD pulled into the car park and rolled to a halt. They clambered out to stretch their legs.

And that was the second mistake they made.

Wee Angus sniffed the air. He started to turn a delicate shade of green.

"Run everyone," he gasped. "Run. Neeps! And they're very close!"

Chapter Twenty Two

The second great battle

Hank McHaggis was still in the caravan when he heard Wee Angus's cry. He had actually been asleep in a corner for most of the time since the battle. This is because og farming is extremely tiring and mentally exhausting and, given the comfort of the rear bunk, he had slept through all the recent adventures. But the cry of 'neep' woke him immediately. He sat up and looked out of the window. The revolting Grabbers' van, dripping with seaweed and mud was parked on the main road. Neeps were pouring out of the back doors and charging across the car park towards the haggises. He could see Hogsnout, Whinjer and Whiner whipping the neeps into a frenzy.

Gofast and Sourpuss (who had had to resort to the deperate strategy of taking wing and flying back from Mull) were directing operations from the roof.

Hank saw at once that the haggises were outnumbered. Unable to reach the door of the Visitors Centre in time, or to retreat to the caravan, they had formed a circle protecting the Thump family…and Gruntfettle's chart!

Hank grabbed his og shooters and an armful of ogs. Loading up, he leapt from the van. The remaining ogs scampered down after him shouting "Me, me, me!" so keen were they to get into the action. Firing from the hip Hank ran towards the massed rank of neeps. "Run for it!" he yelled to the others. "I'll try and draw them off."

The Neeps saw the danger and turned to face him as he let fly with the first ogs. The danger was greater than they knew because, by now, the ogs who hadn't been fed for several days were ravenous. ogs don't need to feed very often but, by golly, when they do …!

Ogs whistled through the air, teeth bared, and plunged into the front ranks. Neeps went down like ninepins as og after og plunged into their midst and started chomping away. It was carnage.

But, in spite of the og feeding-frenzy, there were just too many neeps. Slowly, by sheer force of numbers, they began to press in towards Hank. As the ogs jumped up and down at his feet begging to be loaded and fired, the neeps closed the circle.

"Hurricane!" called Wee Angus. "Grab Drone and drop him on them from as high as you can."

"What!" squealed Drone. "Are you out of your mind. I can't stand heights and anyway…" Before he could say more, Hurricane swooped down and picked him up by the pipes.

"You just get your claws off my pipes you underpowered flying gas-bag," Drone protested as he was lifted up. His cries became weaker and weaker as Hurricane circled higher and higher above the battle.

Watching him go, Wee Angus grabbed the attention of the Huge Haggis and spoke a few urgent sentences.

The HH got the message and grinned.

Several hundred feet above, Drone was trying an appeal to reason. "Okay, Hurricane my old friend," he whined, trying to ignore the sight of all that nothingness between him and tiny shapes below. "Now you're not really going to do this are….yeeeooooww!" His high pitched shriek echoed among the hills as he fell towards the ground. The neeps stopped for a second and looked up at the tiny, shrieking figure as it hurtled towards them. But they could see no danger and turned on the beleaguered Hank once again. Their smell was now so overpowering that he could barely stand.

Caradoc rushed forward, scattering neeps in all directions with his tail as the still wailing Drone rocketed downwards. At the last second, The Huge Haggis barrelled through the gap that Caradoc had made and threw himself on the ground. A split second later Drone landed Splat! right in the Huge Haggis's ample stomach.

"Ooooomph!" gasped HH. "You'll have to lose some weight son, if you're going to make a habit of flying."

"Make a habit of…! Are you out of your mind O Corpulent one?"

Before the Huge Haggis could answer, the neeps turned and charged them. The Great Grunnock, followed by the Thump family flailing fists, feet, handbags (Minnie and PD) antennae (The Grunnock) and hippie beads (Young Kit). Beads? Well anyway, using whatever weapons they could lay their hands on, they joined in the battle. Everyone fought bravely but when Hogsnout, the Grabbers and even Gofast joined in, the tide turned against them. Hurricane and Caradoc were

The ferocious Hairy McHaggis

scooping up ogs by the armful and dropping them into the massed neeps, but they were running out of ammunition. Their hunger satiated, the ogs were becoming lethargic, their little furry eyelids drooping. Neeps lay littered about the battlefield, great chunks gouged out of them, but there were still plenty unscathed. It looked as if all was lost.

Suddenly the ancient haggis battle cry of *'Achnahaaayyy!'* echoed around the glen. Hundreds of haggises were charging down the hillside. In the forefront, waving a huge claymore and leaping over tussocks of heather, was the Hairy McHaggis – one of the most ferocious haggises ever known.

"It worked!" shouted Wee Angus with excitement. "They heard Drone's scream. I knew they would come to our rescue!"

Drone dropped the bloated og he was trying to resuscitate and looked at Wee Angus. After a long pause he simply said: "Oh."

The wave of Haggises, hurling 'the lean and mean team' of specially starved 'fighting ogs', smashed into the neeps with such speed that they were never at risk of falling foul of the stupefying smell. In minutes the battle was over. Fearing for their lives, the Ghastly Grunnock Grabbers scampered back to their revolting van and clattered off as fast as they could, belching huge clouds of black exhaust.

The jubilant victors dispatched the last of the neeps and then greeted the exhausted friends. Wee Angus introduced the Hairy McHaggis (who was actually his uncle).

"Pleased to make your acquaintance," growled the hirsute haggis, managing to make even a polite greeting sound like a declaration of war.

"It's just his way," whispered Wee Angus. "He really likes you."

Mr and Mrs Thump smiled nervously, but Slip took Angus at his word and planted a smacking kiss on Hairy. The haggis's eyes crossed, his schmonker turned bright puce and sparks crackled from his bristles.

"Think you've made a hit there, girl," murmured PD to Slip.

The party went on until dawn.

The Second Great Battle

CHAPTER TWENTY THREE

Punctuation

The next morning the Thumps and friends continued north. There were a few sore heads following the previous night's celebrations and the drinking of copious quantities of 'Frisky'. (This is a special drink made from a centuries old recipe known only to haggises and grunnocks and passed on to very few humans. The author, Colonel Blowen and a certain venerable white-haired ex-Viking are the only known humans who have been told the recipe…all we are allowed to say is that heather, malt, barley, spring water [not a lot of that] and extract of og are just some of the constituents!).

Within the hour they had solved the clue they were after, read the next one and were heading even further north. The desolate Mountains of the Moon rose up on either side as the road wound sinuously through the steep valleys.

Far behind, the UWV clanged, wheezed and groaned its tortuous way after them. Inside, the defeated Ghastly Grunnock Grabbers nursed their wounds. The van was empty of neeps. Not one had survived the onslaught but the smell was still overpowering.

"Maybe a wash would do you lot some good," growled Sourpuss to Hogsnout and his two henchmen.

"Why? It's not December already is it?" whined Whinjer.

"Nah. I think 'e's being personal," whinged Whiner.

Sourpuss sighed. 'You just can't get the henchmen these days' he told himself. Aloud he muttered over and over again "We gotta get that chart!"

Gofast looked uneasy. Time was

Whinjer

running out. If they couldn't get hold of the map then they would be in real trouble. By which he meant serious loss-of-vital-parts trouble at the hands of the Dark and Dingy Ones, the shadowy figures behind Sourpuss.

Belching black smoke and clattering enough to wake the dead, the UWV staggered along the road in the wake of the triumphant Thumps.

"What was that clue again?" asked PD. They were driving down towards a grey and gaunt town. Behind it, the wind whipped across the sea, raising whitecaps.

Minnie loked down at the map. **"Your quest is almost over."**

"Yeees!" Exclaimed the Grunnock loudly from above the sunroof. PD swerved and cast him a quick glare.

"But first you must find the most northerly fellow on the mainland," Minnie continued. **"Don't steal his old money but pinch his apostrophe. Keep it safe and place it well."**

They scratched their heads as they drove through the ancient town and continued up the hills on the other side.

Suddenly Satchmo shouted "Great Grunnocks. I've got it."

The great Grunnock shot his head forward from the caravan window. "You called?" It boomed through the sunroof. PD ducked and sighed in exasperation. They looked at the irrit. "Got what?" they exclaimed in unison.

"The apostrophe, of course," replied Satchmo grinning. "I just caught it. Look." He opened his hand. Nestling inside, shivering with fright was a very small apostrophe. "Hello," It squeaked tremulously.

"Well done, Irrit," said Mr Thump. "Now you look after that and don't get up to any more of your tricks."

Satchmo scowled but nodded. Carefully he placed the little apostrophe in Crunch's hand and, with Thud and Slip they played

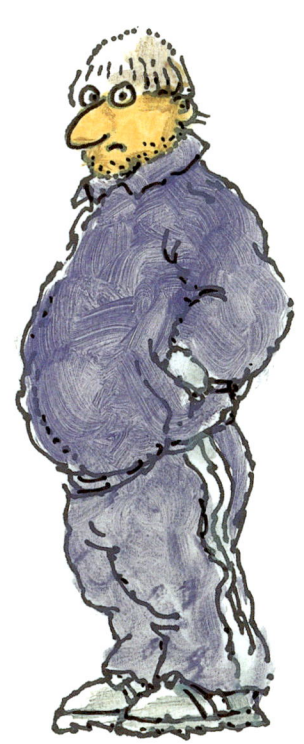

Whiner

A very small apostrophe

The Punctuation Game all the way to the last clue*. Satchmo won with a brilliant move when his double inverted commas surrounded Crunch's new found friend, the apostrophe, and a tetchy exclamation mark that Thud had thrown in.

"We have to go south again now, I think." Minnie was trying to decipher the barely visible writing on Gruntfettle's chart. "I think the map is getting tired."

"I remember now," boomed the Great Grunnock above her. PD gripped the wheel and held her course. "I do wish you wouldn't do that, GG," she sighed. The Grunnock didn't take any notice. Grunnocks rarely do, actually.

"Old Gruntfettle said that each chart only lasts until the last clue for each Stage. It'll probably go up in a puff of smoke soon. Better read it quickly."

Minnie stared hard at the writing. It was fading fast.

"Turning south, you will reach the A9 to Inverness."

"We're on that already," said PD.

"An excursion to find Nessie will take you to a village not far from Urquhart Castle where she is on show. You need the fourth from last letter of the village to complete your collection."

"Well," said Mr Thump. "That sounds possible. Let's go."

Wee Angus, sitting at the back of the caravan nursing a sore head, looked out of the window. He blinked and looked again. Yes, he hadn't imagined it. Far behind, a cloud of black smoke surrounded the Grabbers' UWV. It was moving very jerkily – but it was moving – and it was still following them.

*Rules for the Punctuation Game may be found in a later Stage Booklet.

Chapter Twenty Four

Nessie to the rescue

Alerted by Wee Angus that the Ghastly Grunnock grabbers were still on their trail, The Huge Haggis had called in reinforcements. As the Thumps approached Urquhart Castle they were flanked by two platoons of Haggis–Commandos (fearsome beasties, best avoided if encountered on a dark night in the Highlands after a few drams!), while a squadron of Haggiflyers provided air cover.

A coachload of Japanese tourists who were visiting Urquhart Castle on a three day whistle stop tour of Britain, Ireland, America and The Falkland Islands, couldn't believe their luck. Cameras were readied faster than Hank McHaggis could draw his og shooter. The sudden detonation of flashbulbs convinced Hurricane they were under Ack Ack fire. With a cry of "Tally Ho, strafing run boys!" he led the squadron in a dive on the unsuspecting visitors. og bombs scattered the startled photographers. It was some time before order was restored.

In the meantime PD had driven the car and caravan down to the flat ground beside the castle on the shore of Loch Ness.

Eagerly, they decided to explore the ancient ruins before turning in for the night and making a fresh start in the morning. Their haggis defenders took up station around the castle while Caradoc who had 'seen enough castles in the last 2000 years to last me a lifetime – whatever that might be', turned himself invisible and busied himself raiding the the Japanese tourists' sandwich boxes. Sushi was an interesting new taste sensation. He liked the seaweed best. It reminded him of laver bread and home.

Slip gave the ruins a miss, too. She had her head buried in the road atlas. Every now and again she would refer to a handwritten list of letters and make a note. Soon the notes and crossings-out stretched to several pages, but she stuck to her task.

The coachload of Japanese, with much excited chattering, had decided to lengthen their holiday by a few hours to watch the strange spectacle unfolding in front of them. (This meant they would have to cancel the Falklands trip but they'd find a day to manage that sometime).

In fact quite a traffic jam was building up as more and more cars and coaches stopped to view the vast array of haggises around the castle.

Inside, The Great Grunnock was well and truly lost. It had blundered off down one of the passageways and was now groping in the darkness. Suddenly it saw a faint glow of daylight ahead. It moved forward, slipped on the wet rock and went crashing and tumbling down a slope. With a mighty crunch it ended up against a stone wall. There was a clang of metal followed by the sound of a bolt being slid home.

"Got you," hissed Sourpuss. "Now for the others." Still stunned, the Great Grunnock heard the slap of webbed feet fade into the distance. Then there was silence, broken only by the constant drip of water. The Grunnock rubbed its head. Ouch! A nasty lump suddenly appeared between its snorkel and antenna.

A loud snort broke the silence.

"Who's in here?" called the Great Grunnock nervously.

"And who might be asking," The voice was very deep. It reverberated around the dungeon. GG sniffed. There was a faint but unmistakable scent of fish.

Outside, everybody else settled down for the night. They had looked high and low for the Great Grunnock but, in the end, the Huge Haggis said they must assume it was on special grunnock business.

Young Kit was uneasy. Something wasn't right but he couldn't put a finger on it.

There was a few minutes of bustle while the ogs, who are terribly prone to sleepwalking (sleepslithering, to be accurate), looped themselves into their special sleeping-lead that holds them all together at night and prevents dreamers from wandering off. Eventually, they settled down and gradually the caravan became quiet, the silence broken only by snoring.

Around midnight the door creaked open. Stealthily, Sourpuss crept inside, his feet wrapped in old sacking to dampen the slap of his webs. Stepping carefully over the sleeping forms, he began to tweak Gruntfettle's Chart from underneath Minnie's pillow. She moved and sighed. Sourpuss froze.

Satchmo, who was curled up on Crunch's pillow, felt a tiny splash of water. He glanced up. Above him, the little black cloud quivered nervously. Silently, Satchmo slipped down to the floor. Moving swiftly, he crept up behind Sourpuss. Deftly, he lassooed the duck's tail with one end of the og's sleeping lead.

Holding the chart, Sourpuss crept back out of the caravan. His heart was pounding. He had done it! He had the Magic Map. Now he would get to the Secret Grunnock Grove first! As he waddled up the path towards the UWV parked on the roadside, he didn't notice the long trail of ogs following him. Thinking it was some kind of new neep hunt, the ogs were slithering along silently, grinning in anticipation. The little black cloud saw them. Some sixth sense made it realise that, for once, it could be in the wrong place.

Humming quietly to itself and pretending that it wasn't really there, it slid quietly away. Sourpuss looked up. The moon? He hadn't seen the moon (or the sun for that matter) for years. The duck looked back the way he had come, blinked and felt his webbed feet curl up in sheer terror. At the same moment Wee Angus, who had been woken by Satchmo, leapt from the caravan shouting 'Stop thief!' at the top of his voice. Sourpuss turned to run but the ogs, realising what was happening, charged. Struggling against the furry biting mass, Sourpuss scrambled into the van. At the wheel, Gofast was frozen with shock.

"Move, you idiot!" screamed the duck, plucking ogs from his plumage.

Gofast slammed the van into gear but the UWV had finally suffered enough mishandling. With a tremendous twang, the handbrake snapped and the van careered backwards down the hill towards the loch. As the Thumps and haggises tumbled out of the caravan, the UWV whistled past them. Thud saw Sourpuss's face change from terror to total surprise as, with a puff of blue flame, the magic map disintegrated in his hands, just as the van disappeared under the water.

Seconds later, there was a mighty upheaval as Nessie, with the Great Grunnock riding side-saddle, rose up

Nessie to the rescue.

out of the water. The Ghastly Grunnock Grabbers' van dangled from her mouth. With a contemptuous flick of her head she tossed the battered wreck onto the beach just as a battery of flash bulbs went off. The Japanes tourists' decision to wait had been justified! Nessie grinned at them, waited until the Great Grunnock had stepped ashore then bowed, waved a flipper and disappeared.

As the Ghastly Grunnock Grabbers staggered out of their smashed van, Mole and Bloodhound arrived along with reinforcements, blue lights flashing and sirens blaring. In no time at all, the whole band of villains had been captured and handcuffed.

Checking that everyone was all right, Mr Thump thanked all their haggis helpers and firmly ushered everyone back into the car and caravan. Quickly they drove away from the scene leaving a jubilant Mole and Bloodhound stuffing the unholy Grabber crew into the back of a police van. Mole had surpassed himself, even remembering to bring special webcuffs for Sourpuss.

"Why are we rushing away?" queried Minnie. "We're quite safe now that the police have caught that nasty Sourpuss and his gang."

Mr Thump grinned at Slip. "You tell everyone."

"I've worked out the answer!" Slip proudly announced. "I know where we have to go to find the Sacred Grove and the Grunnock's treasure. But it's some distance away so dad said we'd better get going."

Everyone cheered loudly as they drove off towards Fort Augustus, the first leg of their journey. Behind them a coachload of bemused Japanese tourists looked in surprise at their digital photographs. There was no sign of the Loch Ness monster. All they could see on their pictures was a grinning Welsh dragon filling the frame. Each time their flashes had gone off it had activated Caradoc's materialiser for a split second.

That is why to this day, there are many Japanes tourists who firmly believe that the Loch Ness Monster is a red and green dragon chewing a large leek.

The Thumps have worked out all the clues. Have you?

Finding The Great Grunnock

Once you have found all the clues, you need to put the letters in the correct order. This will make a name of a place marked on all good road atlases. Once you find the dirty deer, you're there. This is the **First Secret Hideaway** of the Great Grunnock.

Here's a tip. It may help if first you can find where a thief from an English county is hiding in Scotland.

Subsequent 'Hunts' will pinpoint other places where the Great Grunnock has found safety on his way to the Secret Grunnock Grove, to find the Treasure.

When you have all the secret places you will be able to find the Secret Grunnock Grove and have a chance of winning the Humungous Grunnock Treasure.

You will also need to collect all the Grunnock Cards. This booklet contains nine. You can get more by ordering **Stage Two of the Grunnock Hunt** directly from St Christopher. (see over)

If your 'tame driver' becomes a 'Friend of St Christopher' (see application form) and protects his or her licence you will get even more Grunnock Cards.

For FLASH GUARD Protection you will receive an extra 6 Grunnock cards and a Secret Grunnock Grove wallchart.

Wallcharts can be purchased separately for £4.99 (Cheque or Postal Order made out to Moods Publishing Company). Send today in the enclosed Order Form and prepaid envelope.

Remember: You can only win the major prize if you are a Friend of St Christopher and have collected all the 144 cards (by purchase or by swopping them with your friends).

Published by The Really Serious Publishing Company Ltd., IOMA House, Hope Street, Douglas, Isle of Man, IM1 1AP. Fax: 01624 681394. Grunnock™ is a trade mark of the Moods Publishing Company.

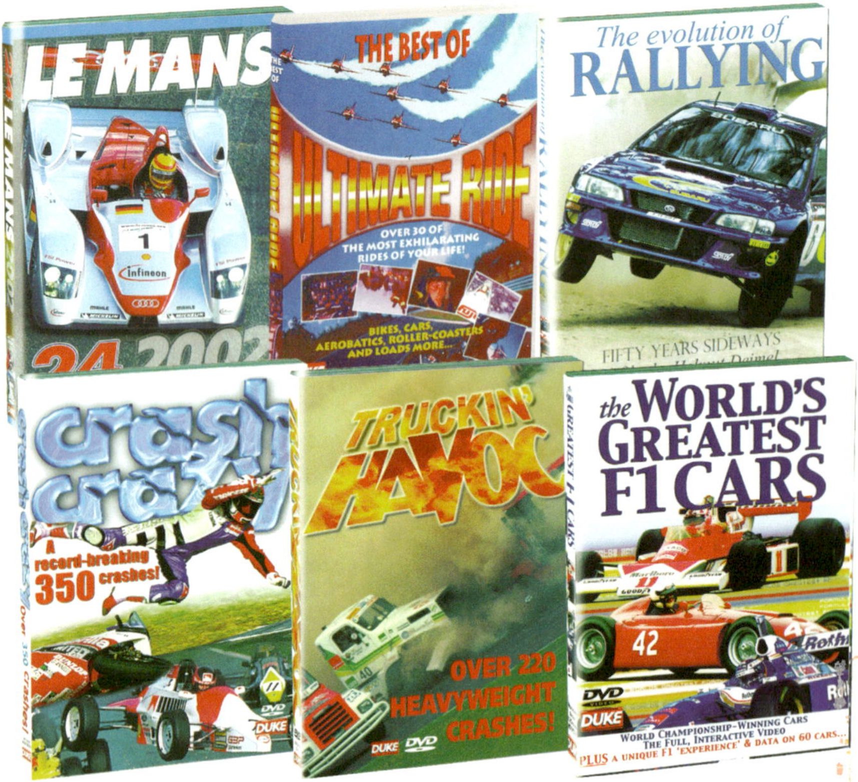